YELLOW SEA

SEOUL
Inchon
Han River
Taejon
Kum R.
Kunsan
Taegu
Samchok
Ullung Island
Pusan
Naktong River
Range
Sobaek
Range
Mokpo
Koje Island
Naktong River
Korea Strait
JAPAN
Cheju Island
Halla-san 6398'

36°
130°
128°
126°
124°

D

KOREA

Land of Broken Calm

The Asia Library

The Asia Library is published in cooperation with The Asia Society, New York.

KOREA

Land of Broken Calm

by

SHANNON McCUNE

DRAWINGS BY KIM FOON

D. VAN NOSTRAND COMPANY, INC.

Princeton, New Jersey

Toronto · London · New York

D. VAN NOSTRAND COMPANY, INC.
120 Alexander St., Princeton, New Jersey (*Principal office*)
24 West 40th Street, New York 18, New York

D. VAN NOSTRAND COMPANY, LTD.
358, Kensington High Street, London, W.14, England

D. VAN NOSTRAND COMPANY (Canada), LTD.
25 Hollinger Road, Toronto 16, Canada

COPYRIGHT © 1966 BY
D. VAN NOSTRAND COMPANY, INC.

Published simultaneously in Canada by
D. VAN NOSTRAND COMPANY (Canada), LTD.

This book is one of the volumes in *The Asia Library*, a series initiated by The Asia Society, Inc., a non-profit, non-political, membership association whose purpose is to help bring the people of America and Asia closer together in their appreciation of each other and each other's way of life.

Library of Congress Catalogue Card No. 66-16903

PRINTED IN THE UNITED STATES OF AMERICA
BY LANCASTER PRESS, INC., LANCASTER, PA.

TO

George Shannon McCune
1872–1941

L. George Paik
1895—

George McAfee McCune
1908–1948

George Blair McCune
1946—

Preface

This book is a personalized account of Korea, the land of my birth. It is written with acknowledged prejudice, for Korea is a land I love and the Korean people are held high in my affections. As a geographer, I see the peninsula as a complex of individual landscapes which may be grouped into regions for better understanding. As a student of Korean affairs, I see the somewhat baffling interrelationships of many historical, cultural, social, political and economic influences that have shaped the totality which is Korea. The aim of the book is a simple one—to help Americans understand better the land of Korea. Korea is a place where Americans have sacrificed lives, have donated services and goods generously, and have shared concern and hope with the Korean people and other peoples in the Free World for freedom and responsible democracy.

One of the recurring problems in writing such an account is the need for proper romanization of Korean sounds. In general, I have followed a system developed three decades ago by two historians, my brother, George M. McCune, and Edwin O. Reischauer; I have omitted the diacritical marks. In the cases of common place names, such as Seoul, of well-known events, such as the *Mansei* movement, and of individual names, such as Park Chunghee, where the person has adopted a different romanization, the McCune-Reischauer romanization is not used. Korean personal names are used in Korean style with the family name (the last name to Westerners) coming first unless the person, such as Syngman Rhee, has adopted the Western style.

PREFACE

As a geographer, I have depended heavily in preparing the
chapters that deal with cultural development on the writings
of others. The book, *The Arts of Korea, An Illustrated History,* Chas. E. Tuttle Company, Rutland, Vermont and Tokyo,
Japan, 1962, by my sister-in-law, Evelyn B. McCune, has been
particularly helpful. *The UNESCO Korean Survey,* Dong-a
Publishing Co., Seoul, 1960, a compilation of many articles
prepared by Korean scholars and translated into English, has
also been very useful in preparing this material. A very useful introduction to the subject of Korean poetry is provided
by Peter H. Lee in his *Anthology of Korean Poetry From the
Earliest Era to the Present,* The John Day Company, New
York, 1964. He has translated many poems into English with
real understanding of both languages. A brief but interesting
book by the same author is Peter H. Lee's *Korean Literature:
Topics and Themes,* published for the Association for Asian
Studies by the University of Arizona Press, Tucson, 1965.

This book has been written during a period of service as
Staff Associate in the Office of the President and as Professor
of Geography at the University of Illinois from February,
1964 to June, 1965. I am indebted to President David D.
Henry, Dr. Joseph A. Russell, Head, Department of Geography, and others who have provided this opportunity for
me to combine research and writing with administrative and
teaching duties. Mrs. Dorothy McAndrews has skillfully translated my scrawl to legible type. Mr. James A. Bier of the Department of Geography has artistically prepared the maps
that accompany the text. I particularly appreciate the pa-
tience and diligence with which my wife, Edith Blair Mc-
Cune, has edited the various rough drafts. She has added im-
pressions drawn from the experiences of her childhood in
Korea.

SHANNON MCCUNE

February, 1966

viii

Contents

I. An Introduction to Korea

Early in the morning in Korea the air often has a special calm and freshness to it. Smoke from breakfast fires rises in undisturbed spirals into the blue sky. In the summer mists hovering over low spots gradually fade away. In the fall hoarfrost slowly melts as the sun warms the land. In the winter crisp, cold air turns one's breath to a sharp white cloud. In the spring cawing crows break the quiet of the morning. In all seasons there is a particular quality to the mornings in Korea that projects hope for a bright new day.

It is this aspect which has been described by the name that has been used for Korea for centuries—Choson—popularly translated, "Land of the Morning Calm." Scholars argue over whether it should be translated thus, or as "morning freshness," or again as the "quiet of the dawn." In any case, for persons who have become sensitive as have the Koreans to the beauty of their land, the name can evoke in their minds the vivid memory of a calm and fresh Korean morning.

1

Koryo is another name used in olden times that is suggestive of the quiet beauty of the land of Korea. Made up of two characters which may be translated literally as "high" and "sparkling," or poetically as "the land of high mountains and sparkling streams," this name has been perpetuated in the Western romanization, Korea. Taehan, a name, modern in the sense of having first been used officially in 1898, and which may be translated as "Great Land of the Han People," is used today in South Korea.

This name, Taehan, gives emphasis to the people of Korea. The Koreans are a distinctive group in the Far East. They have their own language, their own distinctive family structure and society, and their own intimate knowledge of their historical backgrounds. As a people, they came into the Korean peninsula in successive waves of migration—the original groups moving millennia ago, it is believed, out of the forests of Central Asia. During the many centuries which stretch back long before the Christian era and extend into the modern era, racial stock was added by subsequent migrations from China.

The resultant racial and ethnic melding has developed a people who are midway in height between the North Chinese and the Japanese. They are of stocky build with great physical strength and endurance. They can be distinguished facially from their Oriental neighbors by their straight, very dark brown hair, a copper tinge to their yellow skin, high cheek bones and a rather flattened nose bridge. Scholars dressed in distinctive, flowing white robes, ladies in soft-shaded full-length silks, and children dressed in riotously colorful costumes may be seen on festive days when the urge to maintain their Korean customs and traditions is most strong.

Isolated in their peninsula for generations the Koreans have developed a remarkable homogeneity and a great pride in being Koreans. As individuals and as a society they have often undergone privation and hardship. They have had their days of peace and of glory. Though it is dangerous to generalize, many Koreans have a volatile nature. They are quick to take offense when misjudged or maligned, but they are just as quick to laugh and smile at their own mistakes. They are, when unprovoked, a warm-hearted and a calm people, loving nature and their land.

The post-World War II division of Korea, The Land of the Morning Calm, has been a tragedy for the Koreans. Two nations claiming jurisdiction over all of Korea face each other across a wavering Truce Line. Two great armies are poised; two regimes vie with each other to change the traditional economy and society of Korea. The calm of the past has been broken. The Koreans in both North and South long for the day when they can be reunited and continue their development as one nation amidst a society of peaceful nations, a distinctive group in the family of man, and valued contributors to a better world civilization.

The diversified geographic character of the peninsula, the long historical and cultural heritage, the tradition-dominated society and the simple agricultural village economy have been basic ingredients in the complex character of Korea. These have been modified by new forces in recent times: the modernization brought about by Japanese exploitation, the division into Soviet and American zones of military occupation, and the Korean War with its devastation. Today the opposing regimes are engaged in an ideological conflict. The increasingly monolithic Communist state stifles individual freedom in the North. The Republic of Korea, though politically unstable, seeks to preserve freedom for its citizens in the South. To understand Korea it is important to study the underlying characteristics, the modern events that have taken place, and the forces now at work shaping Korea, a Land of Broken Calm.

II. The Land of Korea

Sitting on a hill crest looking out over the hills and valleys of a landscape in Korea one cannot fail to be impressed by both the opportunities and the handicaps which the land of Korea affords its people. They must wrest their living from this land whose supply of livable area, of favorable climate, of natural resources is so limited. Meanwhile, the pressure of more and more people on the land increases. As demands for more intensive utilization of the water, forest, and mineral resources develop, as requirements for large-scale military defense systems take larger shares of the national production, and as the expectation of the people for a more abundant life rises, so also the land of Korea and its potentialities take on significance.

The Strategic Location

Korea is a peninsula set in the heart of the Far East. This simple geographic fact has been the background theme in Korean history. A small nation set among large nations—or, as a Korean proverb phrases it, "a shrimp among whales"—

4

Korea has always suffered when an aggressive force was loose in the Far East. This geographic fact of peninsular location accounts to a significant degree for the present division of Korea. Rather than being a makeweight capable of swinging the balance of power one way or the other, Korea is a precariously split peninsula in which the power struggle is a constant threat to peace not only in the Far East but in the world.

As a peninsula, Korea is attached by a broad, mountainous base to the continent of Asia. Korean storytellers picture their land as a rabbit sitting upright facing China: its ears point northward to Manchuria, the backbone is the eastern mountain crest along the Sea of Japan, and its paws are the peninsulas which extend westward in the Yellow Sea. More precisely, the Korean peninsula extends 600 miles from its northeasternmost point at the bend of the Tumen River (43° North Latitude) to Koje Island off Pusan in southeastern Korea (34° North Latitude). Some 60 miles off the southwestern shore of Korea lies rocky, volcanic Cheju Island; to the east, some 80 miles off the coast of southeastern Korea, lies small Ullung Island. Discounting these offshore islands, the width of the peninsula varies from the broad base along the Manchurian border to a narrow waist of some 120 miles in North Korea. It then widens out, narrows again, then widens once more to roughly 160 miles at its southern end. The total land area is 85,285 square miles—the size of Minnesota. The latitudinal extent of Korea from the Tumen to the southern shore of Cheju is equivalent to the area in the United States that stretches from Massachusetts to South Carolina.

Just as the view from almost any hill crest in Korea abounds in contrast from hill slope to valley floor, so the general pattern of the peninsula of Korea reveals considerable geographic diversity. This is caused by the geologic structure of the land,

5

by the varied climatic influences, and by the manner and intensity with which the Koreans have exploited the land and its resources.

The Land Forms of Korea

Geologically Korea is an "old" land. In north central Korea are exposures of some of the oldest formations of the Archean age. But the complicated geologic history depicts many subsequent upheavals and crustal deformations. In essence, the peninsula is a mass of old granitic rocks. On top of this base and folded down in it along a general southwest-northeast direction are younger series of rock formations which have been metamorphosed through time into gneisses and schists. The trend of these rock formations is similar to those in adjacent areas of Manchuria and the Shantung Peninsula of China across the shallow Yellow Sea. In extreme southeastern Korea there are more recent rock formations which may be correlated with those across the Korea Straits in southwestern Japan.

Relatively recent volcanic action has made its imprint on the geologic structure in only a few places in Korea. Along the northern border of Korea is volcanic Paek-tu-san (san means mountain) which has within it a large crater lake. Lava flows, which cap some of the high elevations in the northern interior of Korea, have welled out from Paek-tu-san and other volcanoes giving some parts of the country a plateau aspect. The volcanic island of Ullung in the Sea of Japan is along a zone of weakness of the earth's crust which extends southeast from Paek-tu-san through an area along the northeast coast and finally ends in Japan. In central Korea on the route from Seoul to Wonsan is "the Iron Plain," an area where lava flows have created a distinctive landscape. On volcanic Cheju Island cone-shaped Halla-san culminates the gradual rise from the coast; it was last active in 1007 A.D. Despite these occurrences of volcanism, Korea for the most part is not underlain with volcanic rock. Most of the rocks, and hence the immature soil bases, are granites, metamorphosed sandstones and limestones, and more recent sedimentary rocks and alluvial material.

In addition to shaping the gross pattern of the land, the geologic past has also influenced some of the local characteristics of the land forms. For example, the granite rocks when exposed to the surface are subject to relatively rapid disintegration and consequent erosion. The results are disastrous, for not only are the denuded, eroded hills difficult to reforest, but the debris from these hills clogs the river valleys and covers good agricultural land.

Korea with its complex geologic history is a land with an infinite variety of rivers and valleys. The earliest Western visitors to the peninsula, the French Catholic fathers who smuggled themselves into Korea, aptly described the appearance of the land as "a sea in a heavy gale." Modern travelers flying over the peninsula by plane are impressed by the infinite number of hills and small valleys, of mountain range after mountain range stretching to the horizon. On the ground no plain is so extensive that one is out of sight of a hill or a mountain in the landscape.

Four-fifths of the land of Korea is made up of hills and mountains, land too rough or too steep for economic cultivation. It is on the plains, the remaining fifth, that the Korean farmer must gain his livelihood. Yet it is from the enduring hills and mountains that he gains an inspiration of beauty and a feeling of stability. Naturally, within the land form patterns there are diversities so that not all Korean farmers have the same physical base for their agricultural pursuits.

The Climate of Korea

Just as the geologic base and the variation in land forms set limits to human activities and give rise to diverse patterns

7

in human occupancy, so the climate of Korea holds a profound influence over the lives of the Korean people. It is a quiet but pervasive influence. It limits, for example, the length of the growing seasons, the amount of water available in the soil and for irrigation, and the direction and character of the winds from which homesteads must be protected. The rhythm of village life, including its festival days, adjusts itself to the weather cycle.

The nature of the climate is caused by the mid-latitude and peninsular location of Korea on the edge of the world's largest land mass—Asia. Located between 34° and 43° latitude, it is affected by a variation during the year in the angle of the sun's rays and, consequently, a decided variation between the cold of winter and the heat of summer. The proximity to the monsoonal center of north Asia, generally centered over Mongolia, results in even more seasonality in the climate. Thus, the winters are colder and the summers hotter than in other regions of similar latitudes away from the continental influence. The monsoonal system results also in a greater preponderance of cold, dry air masses in the weather patterns of the winter months and of warm, moist air masses in the summer or "rainy season."

In common with other areas in these latitudes, the variation in the succession of air masses is associated with weather fronts that pass over the peninsula. There is an old Korean saying: "Three cold (days follow) four warm (days)." The weather of Korea is similar in these variations to the weather of the eastern seaboard of the United States. Like that area, also, in the later summer and early fall an occasional tropical storm (called in Asia a typhoon, from the Chinese word *t'ai feng,* or great wind, rather than a hurricane) sweeps up from the south and curves across the southern part of the peninsula out into the Sea of Japan.

The weather cycle during the year in central Korea reflects

8

the control which is exercised by climatic causants. In January the weather is generally cold and clear. Light snow will stay on the ground. The ponds and streams are frozen. The north winds bite in; radiant-heated Korean floors are a comfort. The cold extends on into February, but by March the weather begins to moderate with only an occasional period of bitter cold. In April warm spring breezes bring delightful days. The winter wheat and barley in central and southern Korea, dormant under the snow blanket of winter, begin to grow again. Farmers work in their fields. The "plum rains," occasioned by the modification of the monsoonal air masses, water the fields and fill the irrigation ponds. By May the land has come alive again. It is not too hot, yet summer-like days become more common. Summer arrives in earnest in June; the days and the nights are hot. The rainy season, flooding the streams and the fields, gives plentiful water to the rice fields. Rains come often in the form of thunderstorms associated with the convectional updrafts of the warm moist air. There is little relief from the heat in August, though the rainfall is somewhat lessened. On a hot day the land seems almost to steam, but the farmers are happy to see the rice growing. September is a delightful month with bright clear days. The rice fields can be drained to bring the rice to fruition. An unpredictable, but fortunately very occasional, typhoon may cause violent winds and heavy rains in central Korea. In the southern fringe of the peninsula along the coast, however, their influence is felt more often. Six or seven may occur in a year, almost entirely in the late summer and early fall. The weather is at its best in October, particularly from the tourists' point of view. The air is clear and crisp, rainy days are few. Fall paints the hills with color, and the sensitive traveler can share with the Korean farmers the fulfillment of harvest days. The golden rice has been cut and threshed; in the south barley is being sowed in the dry fields. Roofs

9

thatched with the newly cut rice straw stand out brightly in each village. In November cold nights and cool days break the usual cycle of four warm days and the winter that has been presaged arrives in earnest in December. Snow flurries frequently cloud skies so that the farmers must take advantage of sunny middays to prepare their fields for winter. Kitchen fires must be kept going all day to warm the floors. Another year has run its variegated cycle of changing weather in central Korea.

Not only is there variation in the climate in Korea throughout the year, but also there is differentiation in the climate geographically in Korea. In fact, each mountain valley and slope has its unique climate. The zones of climatic variation that are dependent upon differences of elevation are in some places very well marked. For example, on the slopes of Hallasan in Cheju Island the differences appear in almost concentric circles. Distribution of vegetation and of crops is easily correlated with the regional climatic differences within Korea, ranging from north to south and from coastal to interior locations.

The Resource Base of Korea

The peninsula of Korea with its diversity of land forms and climate is the stage of natural beauty on which the Koreans have acted out the drama of their history. The land has set limits to the potential of economic development. In the days of a relatively primitive culture, the Koreans used the land only as a base for a hunting and a fishing economy. As the tribal people became settled and began to cultivate the land, growing cereal crops, the population expanded in numbers. Rice, introduced from China, became a major crop which could support large numbers of people. The Korean farmers developed their skills and became the mainstay of a more and more sophisticated economy. In recent decades, particularly under the Japanese (1910–1945), new possibilities were opened up through geologic exploration for mineral resources and through engineering surveys of hydroelectric power potentialities. The conclusion of a survey of the land resources of Korea is obvious: Korea is not a rich land, nor can it support a vastly increased population. However, through wise utilization of their land and resources the Koreans can achieve a rising standard of living.

Wise use of the land must presuppose a peaceful unified country—a condition which does not now prevail. Much of the economic benefit to be derived from the land has to be diverted now to essentially nonproductive defense expenditures in the context of the present relations between North and South Korea and of the threat and tension which exist in the Far East. The resources of the two parts of Korea, when developed in a unified pattern, under conditions of peace, should result in much benefit for both parts. But when hostile regimes are separated by artificial barriers, uneconomic development takes place and both parts suffer.

A greater resource of the Korean peninsula than the land is the people—resilient, energetic, patriotic, volatile, and courageous. The Koreans have sometimes used their land wisely, with due concern for the balance of exploitation and renewal of its resources of land, forest, and water; and at other times they have used it with wasteful profligacy, heedless of the future. They have worked hard on their land; but too often, they have worked their land too hard. Korea is fortunate in having resourceful people who can overcome by diligent perseverance and under peaceful conditions the handicaps of a land not overly generous in natural resources.

For full realization of the land's potential, there is need of balance, both in the exploitation and renewal of its natural and human resources and also in the reinforcing strength that North and South Korea could give each other were they unified.

11

III. The History of The Hermit Nation

The Korean people have a profound respect for the sweep of history which has affected their land. They refer often and with deep feeling to the glories of the past. The tribulations of the present are fatalistically set into a perspective that goes back into the centuries and projects into a distant future. This sense of an inexorable wheel of history has, of course, a relation to their Buddhist heritage, but their respect for history (and the historian) is conditioned, in part, by their Confucian tradition. This historical-mindedness is an important factor in Korean attitudes.

Legendary History

Three or four thousand years ago, the Korean peninsula was inhabited by small groups of people organized in tribes with shifting relationships. These tribes were often isolated from each other in separate valleys and constantly struggled against the rigors of the natural environment in which they lived. They practiced a gathering and hunting economy, with some primitive agriculture. As population pressures increased they moved against their neighbors or migrated ever southward.

The origin of these early Korean people is, of course, not easily determined. However, from their language and some of the customs which have been preserved, they are thought to be descendants of migrants from the forest lands of Siberia. The Korean language, for example, is allied with Tungus languages of central Asia. The ancestors of the Koreans probably moved through centuries from the Siberian forests around or across the Manchurian plain down into the more hospitable, though isolated, Korean peninsula. Another source of pulsating waves of people was North China, by way of southern Manchuria into the peninsula. The mixing of these stocks of people gave the base for the present Korean race, characterized by high cheek bones, noses with flattened bridges, Mongoloid eye folds, straight, very dark brown hair, stocky build, and medium height. Later migrations from central and south China and perhaps northward from southeast Asia had some slight additional influence on the racial character of the Koreans.

The prehistory of the Korean people has been supported by legends handed down by the Koreans for many centuries. Being legends rather than history, they can only suggest the timing of supposed events. However, some aspects of these legends gain credence through the findings of the archaeologist and the prehistorian.

The first, the Tangun legend, reveals the northern origin of the Korean people. According to this legend, Hwanung, a son of the creator of the universe, desiring to be human, descended from heaven in 2333 B.C. He was accompanied by 3,000 heavenly spirits and they made their home on a mountain in northern Korea. A tiger and a bear prayed to Hwanung to give them his secrets. He told them to eat a miraculous wormwood stalk and twenty beads of garlic and stay in a cave for twenty-one days. The tiger, being impatient, left the cave. The bear, however, stayed and then emerged as a beautiful girl. She met Hwanung, who had changed his form, and he "breathed his spirit" on her. Subsequently, she gave birth to a boy, Tangun. Some men of the local wild tribes found the boy under a sandalwood tree and proclaimed him their divinely created king. As king, he taught the barbarians the elements of a new and advanced civilization: cooking by fire, cultivating fields, living as families in houses, obeying their king, and worshiping a single all-powerful divinity.

This, in abbreviated and unadorned form, is the Tangun legend. As told through the centuries, many variations and elaborations have been added. The sandalwood tree detail, for example, was very likely added from the Hindu-Buddhist tradition. Some of the elements are revealing; for example, the bear figures in the symbolism of central Asia and is also found in Ainu tradition in Japan. Monotheism, evidenced in the legend and perhaps going back to sun worship, has continued down to the present day as a characteristic, underlying Korean religious belief.

Another legend, equally revealing of the past, is that of Kija, a Chinese sage. In 1122 B.C., according to the legend, Kija left China with 5,000 followers and came to northwestern Korea. He established his capital at Pyongyang and brought civilization of a comparatively high level to Korea. The Korean people accepted him since he did not come as a warrior but as a scholar, and he and his followers were absorbed by intermarriage. Kija introduced principles of law and government, practices of arts and crafts, particularly working of clay and metal, silk making, animal husbandry, irrigation of rice and other crops, and frameworks of social order, stressing the importance of the family unit. This is a legend, though Chinese histories

14

written long after the supposed event give a great deal of detail in their accounts of it. It does indicate correctly the role of the Chinese migrations as civilizing forces in the centuries before the start of the Christian era.

Recorded history of Korea by Chinese scholar-historians goes back two thousand years to the establishment of a Chinese colony in the area near the present city of Pyongyang in 108 B.C. The colony, called Lolang in Chinese and Nangnang in Korean, had an estimated population, based on tax registers, of 400,000 people. The rich artifacts uncovered by Japanese archaeologists after 1913 from the tombs of the colony reveal a civilization of a high artistic level with some beautiful bronze mirrors, decorated lacquer boxes, and jewelry. These Chinese settlers were eventually absorbed by the Korean population and the Chinese art and architecture they had brought had a profound influence on subsequent Korean cultural development.

The Early Korean People

It is with these legends and these cultural contacts that the Korean people emerged. The Koreans of these early times were called the Han people. (This name is not to be confused with the Han dynasty in China, though the two characters have identical romanizations.) In the north and spreading into Manchuria were other tribes, relatively less stable. The Han people in South Korea had come in successive waves from central Asia. There are some archaeological remains, for example the dolmens, or stone platforms, which some scholars take as evidence of even earlier groups, perhaps of Caucasoid people; but these peoples, if present in Korea, were completely absorbed by the Tungusic Han people who provide the dominant racial stock and the basic language elements of the Korean people. The monotheistic nature worship and shamanism (a mixture of spirit worship and magic) which marked the religious character of these people were also of Tungusic origin.

The Han people were simple agricultural folk who lived in villages and had domesticated animals. The Ma-han were in the southwest; the Chin-han and Pyon-han were in the southeast. There were some differences among the three tribes; the Pyon-han practiced tattooing more commonly; the Chin-han lived in stockaded villages, were fond of music, and mined iron; the Ma-han had many more subgroups with more social equality, grew rice, lived in unwalled villages and used oxen for plowing.

The early Korean people, it is believed, lived in simple agricultural villages and, also, carried on hunting and fishing in the forested hill lands. However, as time went on they became more and more sedentary. Weaving, pottery making and some bronze and later iron work was done for utilitarian purposes, but it had a distinct and simple beauty. Fields were cleared on the plains and simple tillage and production of cereal and vegetable crops were practiced. These people had some cultural contacts with China. The family and clan relationships followed the Chinese patriarchal system.

Being closely dependent upon the land, the early Koreans' folk religious beliefs were closely tuned to a veneration of nature. They recognized a supreme deity. Worship of the deity, and in addition various other gods representing natural elements, merged with belief in good and evil spirits which could be influenced by magical rites. Women who could work themselves into trances and could exorcise the spirits through magic incantations were the forerunners of the sorceresses who still play a significant role in Korean rural society.

The Three Kingdoms and Unified Silla

From the three Han tribes and from other peoples in the north who were more affected by Chinese influence, there developed the Three Kingdoms which dominated the Korean peninsula from 57 B.C. to 668 A.D. (The *Samguk Sagi,* The History of the Three Kingdoms, by Kim Pusik, gives details of the events of these times. It was written long after, in 1145 A.D., and is probably derived from stories handed down by word of mouth.) It was during these centuries at the start of the Christian era in the West that Korea became united as a nation. This unification was not easily accomplished. Only gradually were the different groups welded together, the seagirt boundaries of their peninsular home aiding in this process. There was an influx of cultural influence from China. From Korea ideas—always light baggage—flowed to relatively primitive Japan.

The Three Kingdoms emerged from varied tribal groups. In the north was Koguryo. This kingdom, founded according to legend by a person of divine birth, developed out of the Puyo tribes from the mountain lands of southern Manchuria. The Koguryo occupied an area comprising the Yalu River basin and stretching south through central Korea. In its early days its capital was on the Manchurian bank of the Yalu; later in 427 the main capital was moved to the present city of Pyongyang. The Koguryo absorbed the Lolang colony in 313 A.D. and through the centuries felt the cultural influence of China. However, on their own they developed some interesting art, particularly the tomb murals colorfully depicting scenes of both earthly life and heavenly existence. The history of Koguryo was marked by struggles with tribes in Manchuria and invasions by the powerful Sui and Tang Chinese dynasties. Thus, it was a military state for most of its existence. Early contacts with the kingdoms to the south were limited. However, as Koguryo expanded southward in later centuries it came into conflict with Silla, one of the other kingdoms, and continued to have difficulties with Tang China. Eventually in 668 A.D., after being weakened by wars with its northern neighbors in Manchuria, it was conquered by Silla.

Paekche was the smallest of the Three Kingdoms from the standpoint of military power. Growing out of the Ma-han tribe, Paekche had its first capital near the present site of Seoul. Later the capital was moved south to Kongju and still later farther south to Puyo. Through its ties with Lolang and with states in southern China after the fall of the Han dynasty, Paekche achieved the highest cultural level of the Three Kingdoms. Some of its art forms appear to have been transmitted from the Middle East through China. It also had ties with Japan and as pressure from Silla became strong, leaders and artisans from Paekche migrated to Japan where they were welcomed for the culture and skills they brought. The final dissolution of Paekche was due to a combination of Tang Chinese and Silla forces. Some of the people were taken captive to China, others fled to Japan.

Silla, in southeastern Korea, was economically the most advanced of the Three Kingdoms. Its ruler, also according to legend, was of divine origin, having emerged from a luminous egg. In the valleys of the Naktong River basin and the adjacent Kyongju plain, sedentary agriculture with crops of rice and other cereals gave a firm base to the economy. The raids of pirates from Kyushu in Japan wrought devastation from time to time, but generally Silla lived in peace. Tombs of early kings which have been excavated had in them many beautiful crowns, buckles, and other ornaments of soft gold, in some cases decorated with jade and colored glass. Some of these indicate ties with art forms and wearing apparel of central Asia and even farther west. Silla absorbed Paekche and with the aid of Tang China, conquered Koguryo, thus gaining political control over the entire Korean peninsula. One troublesome area on its border was a small kingdom, Karak, near the present area of Pusan. From time to time, Karak

18

(called Mimana by the Japanese) was a beachhead for the Japanese, though in much of its history it was a dependency of Silla which in 562 finally absorbed it.

During this period of the Three Kingdoms Korea became more civilized. Prior to and during the early part of the period the people had a primitive fishing, hunting, and gathering economy, and were organized into tribes or kingdoms. One of the most significant of the cultural events was the introduction and spread of Buddhism. It came into Koguryo in 372 A.D., and shortly afterward was introduced in Paekche (384), and later in Silla (424), though it was another hundred years before it became firmly established there. This religion, originating in India, had gone through a major metamorphosis in China. The Buddhist sects which came to Korea from China brought a civilizing force to the wild tribes. The major sects were devoted to the veneration of the Buddha, often depicted in sculpture with a beatific smile and in a graceful pose. The Buddhist beliefs in a cycle of life, culminating in a paradise to which the good would go, gave a sense of purpose to the primitive Koreans. In its early days Buddhism captured their hopes and quieted their fears. Associated with Buddhism in Silla was a way of knighthood, the *hwarangdo*. This appears to have been, in part, a military code with training programs in swordmanship, but the martial arts were to be used in protecting the weak.

Buddhism became well entrenched in unified Silla during its days of glory from 668 to 935. Monasteries, particularly of the Hwaom sect which venerated a creative Buddha, were established in the vicinity of Kyongju, the capital. The Buddhist-inspired art of Silla was marked by bas-reliefs in caves, statues in shrines, simple but grandeur-filled temples, and associated pagodas. The Silla also fostered science, as evidenced by a stone observatory, and the arts, as evidenced by dances and songs. Literature, written in a makeshift ortho-

19

graphic system to bridge the gap between classical Chinese and Korean, was highly valued.

Silla was not able to maintain control over all of the peninsula. Japanese pirates continued to raid the east and south coasts. In defense, the Koreans had built their towns five miles or more inland. When pirates landed, the Koreans circled and burned the invaders' boats, thus marooning them on the land. In the northeast, marauding tribes from Manchuria raided the villages of the sedentary farmers. In the northwest, on both sides of the Yalu River, there was little permanent settlement. It was a "march" between Silla with its center far to the south and Tang China.

Silla profited much from its nominal vassalage to the Tang dynasty which had helped them subdue Koguryo. They copied some of their governmental forms from Tang China. Confucianism as an ethical way of government was introduced from China along with the idea of examinations for civil service. Agricultural production was greatly increased. Families with great land holdings built large houses, almost palaces, in Kyongju and constructed elaborate tombs for their ancestors. The court received envoys from China. Even Arab traders knew and wrote of the wealth of Silla. Korean scholars studied in China and one Korean monk made a holy pilgrimage to India. The city of Kyongju had a million inhabitants and was one of the great cities of the world of that time.

The Koryo Dynasty

The detachment from life, which was characteristic of Buddhism, and the rivalry among the monasteries weakened the political power of Silla. The Tang dynasty had come to an end in 907 leaving confusion in northern China. In 935 a Korean general, who had achieved virtual control over the northern area of Korea in 918, led a revolt which overthrew the Silla dynasty without violence. The new kingdom, Koryo, had its capital in west central Korea at the present city of Kaesong, forty miles northwest of Seoul.

Koryo started with a strong militant aspect. Much effort was expended in subduing the tribes in the northeast. The "march" on the Yalu continued to guard that frontier. Within the peninsula the political organization that was developed in the Silla period, to divide the land into provinces, counties, towns, and villages, was maintained with some modifications. The Confucian pattern of government, including the examination system, continued but without much vigor. Buddhism with its ramifications of landholding monasteries remained the state-established philosophy. A meditative sect, Son (Zen in Japanese), was introduced from China in 1097, and eventually became the most powerful of the five major Buddhist sects.

The arts flourished in Koryo. Of enduring value was the inlaid celadon pottery with its distinctive green-grey color. Families in certain villages made this pottery, using techniques adopted from China which were, in turn, given distinctive Korean treatment. The geometric floral or bird patterns were inlaid to show through the hard celadon glaze. Many of these pieces were preserved in tombs and exquisite examples are now displayed in art museums around the world. Printing from wooden blocks helped disseminate Buddhist sacred writings. Soon, reusable metal type was developed (long before Gutenberg) and employed in printing not only the religious writings but also other materials for the increasing number of scholars and schools in the peninsula. The greatest artistic works were Buddhist-inspired: temples, stone pagodas, and religious figures of varied sizes and composition. The great cultural advances made by the Koryo Kingdom were interrupted, however, by periods of decline due mainly to outside invasions.

Japanese pirates along the coasts continued to raid and

21

harass Koryo, but the dominant outside forces were the tribes which sprang from the plains of Manchuria and Mongolia. These well-organized forces, in sweeping into China, protected their flanks by subduing Koryo. The first were the Chi-tan who invaded the peninsula in 1011 and in 1014 burned the capital. Their influence was limited, but the Mongols, who came two centuries later, left their mark. The Koryo king fled to the island of Kangwha, near Kaesong, where the court remained in refuge from 1232 to 1270. Here the narrow straits furnished protection from the horse-riding Mongolian warriors, but with his land overrun the Koryo king eventually submitted himself to the Mongols. His successors were forced to take Mongol princesses for their wives and adopted many of the customs of their conquerors. The widespread contacts of the Mongols with the Middle East and even Europe brought cultural innovations to Korea. Social structure was modified with more mobility for people to rise through the Buddhist or military hierarchy. Not only did the Mongols control Korea, but Kublai Khan used the peninsula in 1274 and again in 1281 for invasions of Japan. The Kamikaze, or Divine Wind (in actuality, devastating typhoons) saved Japan at this time and resulted in great losses among the Korean sailors and soldiers who were impressed into Mongol service.

During the later part of the Koryo period, a new force, neo-Confucianism, made a profound impact on Korea and the Koreans. The Buddhist monks had become decadent and influenced by Lamaism, a variant form of Buddhism. They had failed to provide moral and spiritual leadership. The Buddhist monasteries with their large land holdings demanded more and more from the farming population. The monks' and abbots' close associations with the hated Mongols are said to have further estranged them from the Korean people. Thus, Korean scholars who brought back from China a new version of Confucian philosophy, that of Chu Hsi, were able to fill a philosophical void.

The world, according to the dominant Korean philosophical school of Chu Hsi Confucianism, was controlled and inspired by a Supreme Ultimate. At the same time there were moral laws with ethical standards by which man could regulate his conduct. Benevolence, righteousness, propriety, wisdom, and commitment were the major virtues which man should cultivate through personal study, reflection and intuition. This philosophy combated the decadent features of Buddhism and through belief in a divinely ordered world provided a viable religious substitute. It gave place and prominence to the scholar-leaders, who had been stifled in the atmosphere of the court or of the monasteries. In their schools, often located away from the court in the provinces, the new ideas flourished. The freeing of the mind which was fostered by this neo-Confucian doctrine was matched by a desire for the freeing of the society from the baneful effects of Buddhism. Thus, neo-Confucianism played a significant role in the overthrow of the Koryo dynasty.

The Yi Dynasty

In 1392, a remarkable general, Yi Songke (who later became Yi Taejo in his posthumous or throne name), with the assistance of the Ming dynasty, which had replaced the Mongols in China, founded a new dynasty, the Yi. This ruled Korea for the next five centuries. Confucianism of the Chu Hsi version was adopted as the state philosophy. Patterns of government based on the Ming legal code were adopted. The court copied Ming costumes for their dress. A land reform benefited the new scholar-official class and the retired soldiers who were able to settle in the pioneer northern areas. One of the notable achievements was the invention of a new written language based on simple phonetic symbols. This was "given" to the

23

common people in 1446. Coupled with the spread of printing using movable metal type, it gave promise for widespread literacy and learning. Buddhism was isolated into monasteries and was no longer a dominant political force. The court was reorganized along classical Confucian patterns; the local government of scholar-magistrates and provincial governors gave political order throughout the peninsula. The Buddhist-inspired art of sculpture declined, but new arts of calligraphy and landscape painting began to flourish. These skills belonged particularly to those of the scholar class who had the leisure to pursue them.

The Yi dynasty was not without its troubles. The population had grown and, though there were pioneer lands in the north, population pressures were felt in the south. The land was used intensively with a high amount of human labor supplemented by work animals and simple implements. Crops were dependent upon the vagaries of climate; irrigation systems were small and only served as adjuncts to the rainfall in supplying water. The village life was quite self-sufficient. Education for the masses was limited. The scholar-landlord class, the *yangbans,* only a small percentage of the people, dominated the officialdom and the economy. Some of them established schools in rural areas, but these were for the children of the scholar class, rarely for the common people. Forest lands were owned by the crown and were not well managed, insect blights creating havoc from time to time. Roads were primitive. The provincial capitals were towns rather than cities. Seoul, the capital newly built after the start of the dynasty, was the only real city. It derived much of its economic well-being from the court and powerful families who, in turn, gained wealth from their lands in the provinces.

Because of its close ties with Imperial China, the turmoil and invasion there affected Korea. The Japanese, under Hideyoshi, launched in 1592 an invasion through Korea aimed

24

at China. This was halted with Chinese assistance, but only after six years of great devastation. A Korean hero, Admiral Yi Sunsin, using ironclad ships was able to cut the Japanese supply lines. The Korean peninsula was well adapted to guerrilla warfare. (It is interesting to compare the military actions of 1950–51 with those of this invasion; the ground routes taken and some of the strategic moves have remarkable parallels.) The Korean people think back on this period with bitterness, for it was a time when their towns were destroyed, and famine and disease took a heavy toll. Hatred of the Japanese was aroused then and has been perpetuated through legends, stories, and childhood games.

Even after the withdrawal of the Japanese and the Chinese (both sides had looted extensively) peace and prosperity did not come, for the Manchus grew to power on the plains of Manchuria. After driving the Ming court from Peking they sent an invading force into the Korean peninsula to punish the Korean kings who had misguidedly but loyally given support to the Ming dynasty. The Manchus quickly adapted themselves to Chinese traditions. Once again Korea accepted its role as a "younger brother" nation, this time to Manchu China.

After these many invasions the Koreans sought the seclusion of a hermit nation. They attempted to close their frontiers. The Japanese were allowed a trading post near the present city of Pusan, but contacts were kept to a minimum. Some envoys were sent on missions to Japan where they were welcomed for the new ideas they brought on methods of government. The Yalu River basin was kept as a no-man's-land to protect the northern border. Tribute was sent periodically to Peking in the Confucian tradition of the tributary state, and scholars wandered to China for study. Generally, Korea kept her borders sealed, especially against the new religion, Christianity, whose missionaries occasionally smuggled their way into the peninsula. Some scholars, however, brought back new (or Western) learning from China and beginnings were made in scientific and mathematical studies.

If, during the ensuing period of relative seclusion, the efforts of the Korean people could have been devoted to internal development, Korea would have emerged as a strong, though small, nation. But economic and social development was not forthcoming. The military defense system was allowed to deteriorate; there was almost no military training. So-called military officers were actually scholars holding sinecure positions. New agricultural techniques and new crops were largely ignored. The villages continued on their self-sufficient ways.

The court and the scholar class became more and more estranged from the common people. Within the court factions of scholar-officials feuded between themselves. The growth of factionalism is a peculiar phenomenon in Korean social history. Its causes are varied and may be related to the isolation and diversity afforded by Korean geography, to the rigidness of Confucian political thought, to the fanatic loyalty given the family rather than the state and society. Korea thus was a weakened nation with a false concept of the strength of its "elder brother," China. The hermit nation was ill-equipped to face the world when its doors were opened through recognition of Japan in 1876.

In the Far East at the close of the last century, Japan, revitalized politically and militarily, was growing in power. Weakened China could not under its archaic government structure provide the stabilizing counter-force which it had exerted for centuries. Czarist Russia sought to develop its Far Eastern possessions and to emerge as a strong force in the Pacific. European nations were interested in encouraging Far Eastern trade for their industrializing economies. The United States was awakening to an awareness of its neighbors far across the Pacific. Korea, its court riven with dissension, was caught in the midst of all of these countervailing forces.

Modern History

Japan defeated China in 1894–1895, in a war where the first shots were fired in Korea. Ten years later Japan went to war with Russia. While Korean independence was ostensibly guaranteed, sea battles were fought around Korea and the peninsula was used for movement of Japanese forces into Manchuria where decisive land battles were fought. Having sent troops into Korea, Japan did not withdraw but gained further controls, declaring a virtual protectorate over Korea in 1905. This was a complex period in Korea's history. Having lost the support of Imperial China, the Korean court was weak and vacillating. The common people had no leadership and were stunned by the rush of modernization. Outside powers, rather than assisting, intrigued against each other with Korea a pawn in their dealings. Finally, in 1910 Korea was annexed outright to Japan, the Korean royal family was made a part of the Japanese imperial system, and Japan quickly followed political control with economic domination.

The years as a Japanese possession from 1910 to 1945 were difficult ones for the Korean people. The Japanese ruled with a harsh hand. They forced economic development, which brought many new ways to Korea. Most of the benefit of this changing economy, however, went to the Japanese and the handful of Koreans who collaborated with them. New mining enterprises, development of hydroelectric power potentials, a vast network of roads, a strategic and economic-based railroad system, growth of cities and industrial centers, all served to transform Korea. Agricultural production was greatly increased, in part, to supply rice to the growing cities of Japan. At the same time a population explosion of serious dimensions was taking place, so that the mouths to be fed more than matched the available food for the Koreans.

New Japanese laws and social customs were introduced, but because they did not have the weight of Korean moral and social sanctions behind them they were not wholly accepted by the people. Thus, the Koreans became almost an amoral people, for their old laws were not enforced and the new laws were not truly accepted. In answer to their groping for belief, Christianity offered to many a religion to which they could commit themselves. Of all of the lands of Asia, Christian missionary work was most successful in Korea, though even here only one-twentieth of the people became Christians. The government-controlled educational system which might have built a moral base for the people was instead designed, in the words of a high Japanese official, so that "the Koreans should be taught to follow, not to know."

World War II had little physical effect on Korea except for further serious economic exploitation. The Japanese in launching their moves against Manchuria in 1931 and against north China in 1937 used Korea as a supply base. Koreans followed in the wake of the Japanese conquerors as laborers and petty merchants. Uprooted and without high moral standards, these Koreans gained a deservedly poor reputation in the Japanese-occupied lands of China and Southeast Asia. Many had migrated to Japan to provide unskilled workers in Japanese war industries. Korea's minerals, notably coal and iron, and agricultural products provided some of the raw materials for Japan's war machine. Koreans were not trusted in the Japanese army, but did provide work battalions. Though Korean hatred of the Japanese was not quelled, there was no fifth column in Korea, for the Japanese held firm control.

It was this land which welcomed its freeing from the Japanese at the end of World War II with great jubilation. Korean hopes for immediate independence were, however, dashed when they discovered that Korea had been divided by an arbitrary line, the 38th parallel, separating American and Soviet zones for the purposes of the acceptance of the surrender of Japanese forces. The subsequent events: the continuance of the dividing line, the varied policies in each zone, the setting up of rival governments, the Korean War with its devastation, the long uncertain truce period (still existing), the continued divergent political developments in the north and the south, have shattered the unity of the land and the hopes of the people.

Still a sense of history is a paramount factor in the life of the average Korean. He looks to the past to guide him in the future. The legends, the relics of the old kingdoms, the cultural ties with the past are vivid in his mind today.

IV. The Traditional Korean Way of Life

Besides the profound love for their land and deep respect for their long history the Korean people also have an emotional attachment to their traditional way of life. Yet characteristic Korean society has undergone great changes in recent decades. The old ways in their totality will never return. Many Koreans look upon their past society with nostalgia, glossing over in their memories or accounts of it many of its evils, remembering only its good features and giving to it an aura of perfection which never existed.

Korean society developed over many centuries. Many of its features had their origin in China, but in Korea they were adapted and changed. The result was a society with certain major characteristics: the central importance of the family, the distinct role of the scholar-landlord, the aloof position of government, the intimate character of the agricultural village attuned to the limitations of the good earth and the cycle of seasons, and the emotional outlets furnished by secular and religious festivals. The visible personal characteristics deriving from this society are found in the language, dress, and food of Korea.

Language

The Korean language was developed from a Tungusic linguistic base going back into the distant past when the Korean ancestors were in central Asia. To it were added many words from Chinese. The Korean language is marked by a variation based upon the place in society of the speaker. For example, social equals will use one set of verb endings and certain special words in speaking to each other; superiors will use simplified "low talk" to inferiors; inferiors will use "high talk" with numerous honorifics when speaking to superiors. The classical written language used by the Korean court and scholars was Chinese, just as Latin was used for centuries in Europe. To the classical Chinese, verb endings and connectives were added, with Chinese characters borrowed for the Korean sounds. However, in the early days of the Yi dynasty, a remarkably effective alphabet, phonetically based, with twenty-eight simple symbols, was invented by a group of scholars commissioned by the king. This script, later called *hangul* and further simplified, was easy to learn, but being phonetic did not have the precision of the Chinese characters. So a mixed script was developed combining Chinese characters with hangul. The resulting Korean written language is rich in its ability to express thoughts both concrete and abstract.

Dress

The traditional Korean dress has undergone modification through the centuries. In recent decades, more and more Koreans have been adopting Western-style clothes. The use of school and military uniforms both under the Japanese and more recently has been accelerating this trend. Among the well-to-do and in the conservative rural areas the Korean costume of the past has continued to be used. For their traditional dress, white is the universal color. Perhaps originally

31

it was a mark of mourning which became standardized as people extended their use of mourning clothes for members in lateral branches of the family and for longer periods of time. Keeping the white clothes of the family clean is a time-consuming task for Korean women. Greys and blues, not showing dirt so easily as white, are often used, particularly for outer garments.

The style of clothes was developed over the centuries, but shows particular influence from the period of the Ming dynasty in China. Obviously, there are differences, depending upon the social status and occupation of the wearer. In the traditional style, the men wear wide baggy trousers, tied at the waist and gathered at the ankle. Jackets are short and loose and tied with a single bow, which is a unique feature of Korean dress. A short vest with pockets is worn over the jacket. Completing the outer costume, particularly for formal wear, is a long, flowing coat, also tied with a bow. The old-style hats of the men were made of lacquered horsehair with a narrow brim and high crown to fit over the customary topknot. Traditionally, the headpiece was of three parts—a binding which kept the topknot erect, an inner hat of softer horsehair, and then the stiff outer hat. These are seen only rarely today. Though stockings are shaped to the right and left feet, the shoes, made of leather and cloth for formal wear or of straw for farm use, are interchangeable. Clothing varies with the seasons. In the summer the garments are usually thin and highly starched, in the winter they are padded. Cotton is the common cloth, though hemp is used for mourning, and silk is used for the facing of the vest and, by the rich, for the other garments.

Women, dressed in the traditional style, wear a long pleated skirt over loose trousers that are shaped but not tied at the ankle. Their inner jackets are short and bound tightly over the breast. The outer jacket is looser, sometimes fastened with ornamental buttons, though more usually with the single bow. They do not wear vests. The women sometimes wear a cloak, although regional customs vary. Country women wear cloths tied around their heads. They wear their hair long, gathered into a bun at the neck or plaited into braids that are looped around the head. Again, regional ways of wearing and covering the hair vary. Modern city women rarely wear hair coverings and many of the younger ones have cut their hair. Traditional white is sometimes varied with soft grey or other subdued tones. Silk is restricted mainly to the wealthy women. It is in the larger cities, as all over the world, that the pace of fashion is set. Here one sees ladies beautifully gowned in brocade skirts of exquisite pattern and jewel-like colors.

Children on festival days or at New Year's may, in traditional style, wear clothes which are similar in design to those of adults, though boys rarely wear vests and outer coats are not worn. The color is much gayer for such occasions. A distinctive feature is the jacket with sleeves made of narrow strips of various bright colors or satin woven that way. In the modern day, drab, dark, and utilitarian uniforms are worn universally by school children.

Food

Korean food, naturally, is based upon the available agricultural and marine products. Rice is a universal and desired element in every meal; in fact, the Korean word for food is rice. However, many Koreans cannot afford rice and must use barley, grain sorghum, or millet as a substitute. This is particularly common in the north. Along with the rice or some other cereal the Koreans eat small quantities of meat and dried fish. Chickens and eggs form an important supplement to the diet. Soup with vegetables and flavored with meat or fish is often used as a main dish with the steamed cereals. A unique part of the diet and important for its vitamin content is *kimchi,* an unbelievably "hot" pickle. Recipes vary but they usually contain Chinese cabbage, long white radishes, red peppers and other vegetables with ample garlic flavoring. The home diet is simple; restaurant and festival dishes are much more elaborate and highly seasoned. Fruits, such as apples, pears, small melons, persimmons, are eaten in season. Regional differences add variety to the diet; for example, fish, both fresh and dried, are more prevalent in the diet along the coasts.

The characteristic food, clothing, and language of the Korean people set them off from other ethnic groups in the Far East. In this modern period some of these distinctive characteristics are disappearing or being modified. For example, in South Korea, American slang phrases have entered the daily language with pronunciations sounding exotic to the ear of the visitor. Western dress, easier to keep clean and to be mass-produced in factories, is fast replacing the traditional garb. Canned foods are beginning to be used more commonly. In South Korea the import of American grains, dried milk, and other food for relief and school lunch programs has brought about great changes in the diet.

The Korean Family

The Korean society is based very firmly on the family. The relations between the family members give valued continuity and place to the individual. This importance of the family is derived from ideas coming from China and modified in Korea. It is interesting to speculate as to what might have happened if a feudal system with loyalty to a lord of a district (as did develop in Japan) had been developed in Korea. Fundamentally, the Confucian system of "correct relations" of superior-inferior status between husband-wife, father-son, older brother-younger brother, older friend-younger friend, and ruler-subject is the basis for Korean personal relationship. This is a rather rigid hierarchal system which emphasizes

34

the past and is not too well fitted for transition to a modern world.

The essential social unit in Korea is the single family of husband, wife, and children. The oldest son and his wife live with the family and continue on the family line. Daughters, when married, leave the family to join the family of the husband. The younger son after his marriage may be set up in a separate family, but will continue to maintain relations in a subordinate position. The male-dominated family is thus extended. In the old days, marriages were arranged by the parents usually with the assistance of a go-between. The lineage of prospective brides was studied with care. Detailed family registers were maintained, so that intermarriage might not occur. In the traditional way of life, the horoscopes of the young couple were also analyzed to assure propitious marriages which would result, hopefully, in sons to carry on the family line. These customs have been rapidly changing with the modernization of Korea and the accordance of more freedom to women.

In the home the father is the dominant figure. He is given obedience by his wife and children and his word is law. The new bride of the eldest son who joins the family has a hard life as she undergoes training and sometimes abuse by her mother-in-law. After the birth of her first son, if she is so fortunate, this situation is eased. The mother plays a quiet, but often powerful, role managing the household and taking care of the children. This role increases almost in direct proportion to the number of sons and subsequent daughters-in-law she may have. The boys, particularly the first-born, are much favored over their sisters. They are given opportunities for formal education, for example. In various other ways, such as in the serving of food, the male members of the family have the preference. They are served first and eat separately, the women then eat, the daughters and daughters-in-law being last. The grandfather, when he reaches the age of sixty, usually retires from active management of the farm and business affairs, though he still is revered and his advice followed. The grandmother looks after the young grandchildren and continues to dominate her daughters-in-law.

This traditional system of hierarchy, though it had its evils particularly for the young women, had its strength in maintaining harmony within the household. The family was usually a happy place, particularly in times of prosperity. Through the interlinkage of families work could be exchanged. When fortune smiled upon one family, through a bright son, for example, who passed examinations and became an official, or through bountiful crops, all of the interrelated families shared in the good fortune.

Because of the interfamily connections the Korean family is part of a larger grouping or clan. This term, clan, is somewhat misleading when applied to Korean social structure for it may denote to the Westerner a very close relationship. Actually, the clan connections in Korea are not too rigid. The extended family will identify itself with a place of origin, the Kims of Andong, for example. Relations between families in the clan are more or less ceremonial and for purposes of identification rather than control, though some families whose lineage is more direct to the founder of the clan will be accorded deference by other families. The family names, which come first in Korea as in China, are limited in number. The most common, for roughly one in five, is Kim, meaning gold; other common names are Yi or Lee, Pak, Chang, Cho, Han, Chae, Yu, Hong, Hwang, and Sim. Following the family name comes the generation name so that brothers, for example, may all have the same second name. Finally, there is the personal name which is chosen with care to relate in meaning or in the form of the written character with the characters for the other two names. Children are often called by nicknames, sometimes

36

of a purposely derogatory nature so that evil spirits of sickness will not be attached to the child. Scholars and artists often use poetic names to sign their works.

The Korean Village and Home

Korea was for many centuries a land of villages, many of them being made up of families of one clan. The wives were brought from neighboring districts so as not to have intermarriage within the village. In traditional Korea the village was a self-sufficient unit based upon an agricultural economy. Houses were clustered together with a common well and washing place, a common stone grinding wheel, and often in South Korea a large tree venerated as a place of good spirits. The village was usually located along the contact line between the plains and the hills where it could be sheltered from the prevailing winds. The houses had courtyards and stone and mud fences for protection from wandering animals. Paths led from the village to the fields and to the hill lands where brush, wood, and grass could be gathered. Roads for wheeled carts led to main roads, which fed in turn in a radial pattern to a town. The towns were, in reality, overgrown villages made different by the presence of a market place, governmental offices, and perhaps a school or gathering place for scholars.

The Korean rural homestead is built around a small courtyard. On sunny days this sheltered place is used as a work and living place by the family. Children play their games here and women clean and cut vegetables or mend clothes. The threshing and drying of grain and the repairing of farm implements are carried on in this protected open space. Tool sheds, chicken coops, storehouses, and a shed for a cow are ranged along both sides of the courtyard. A simple gate leads through a wall that encloses the third side with the house forming the rest of the rectangle.

A house in an agricultural village is made of simple local

materials—stones, wooden beams, mud plaster, grain sorghum or reed stalks, and rice straw thatch. In some localities where it is in abundant supply, slate takes the place of straw for roofing material. In the forested northern interior of Korea, wooden shingle roofs are common. The homes of the scholar-landlords or the wealthier farmers are roofed with tile rather than thatch and so are easily distinguishable in a village.

The rural house is simple in its construction. Large, rough-shaped stones at each corner of the two rooms and sometimes at the midpoint of the outer walls form the foundation. Earthen walls are built up to the height of the foundation stones. Along this base, timbers, preferably of insect- and rot-resistant red pine, are laid. The upright timbers, six or seven feet in height, are then set into these and cross timbers are set at the top. These timbers are customarily mortised together with wooden pegs, though iron spikes are now being used more commonly. Between these wooden frameworks a wicker-work of grain sorghum or reed stalks is woven. Then mud mixed with rice straw is plastered over this base. In wooden frames cut into the wicker-work are hung latticed wooden doors which are covered with light-filtering paper. Between the rooms similar lattice doors that slide are placed. A center ridge pole is placed on beams erected at each end of the house. From this ridge pole lighter poles extend down to the top timbers of the walls and out to form eaves of two or three feet. Under the front eaves a wooden veranda may be built. On roof poles a thatch made of rice straw is laid and tied in long strips which overlap enough to give a tight, waterproof roof. Every year, if possible, a new coating of thatch is laid so that over the years the roof becomes increasingly tight and waterproof.

The kitchen room, earthen floored, is built at a lower level at one side of the house. The stoves, iron kettles placed in a crude covered fireplace of stones and mud, are built along the inner wall of the kitchen. Careful stoking of the fire enables the Korean housewife to cook rice that will rival any recipe in the world. The smoke and heat from these stoves goes through rock-lined channels under the floor of the house and out a chimney at the far end, furnishing a system of radiant heating that is unique and ages old. In the heat of the summer cooking is done outside on a temporary stove and the kitchen and the floor flues are not heated. But in the cold winter season the heated floor is a great boon. Honored guests are usually given "the hot seat" near the kitchen wall.

The inside of a Korean house is simple. The floors of the rooms are made of mud that is packed around and above the flues. This is then usually covered with oiled paper. Shoes are not worn in the house for the Korean sits and sleeps on the floor. The inside mud walls are commonly papered, in the poorer homes with any sheets of newspapers or magazines that can be found. There is very little furniture. Wooden chests, often brass-bound, are used to store the sleeping pads and quilts which are spread on the floors at night. The homes are small, but remarkably functional.

Class Structure

Class differences are to be noted in Korea, many of them due to differences in occupation. The majority of the people are the farmers. They, along with the fishermen and the wood gatherers in the mountain lands, are the base of the economy and the society. Often farmers engage in fishing and woodcutting as a seasonal or part-time activity. In early times below this large class of farmers, which occupied a lowly but honorable place, were a small number of low caste folk—the butchers, the sorcerers, and the landless laborers. There were some people who were actually little more than slaves, but might more properly be classed as destitutes. They lived off

39

the bounty of the well-to-do and gave service in return for subsistence.

Above the farmer class were a small number of yangbans, the scholar-landlord class, who had close ties with the government and the court. They were bound by tradition, often had rural estates to which they could retire, but spent most of their life in the provincial capitals or in Seoul. They lived off the rents from their lands tilled by tenants and were the only ones who could afford concubines or servants. They had leisure to engage in the arts. Their sons would be educated in the classics, rather than work in the fields. If he came on bad times a scholar could attach himself to some better situated relative and be a teacher in a village or town school. Yangbans held to traditional clothing and ways of life. The women of these families were kept in relative seclusion and were trained, for example, in the gentle ways of silkworm rearing and weaving. They did not work in the fields and they had servants for their household chores. The men sought to become officials and, if successful in the examinations, were able to protect their land holdings and their class status by use of their official positions. Their homes were marked by greater elaborateness and size as well as by tile roofs. Their weakness was that they tended to be a somewhat parasitic class, estranged from the common people.

There was some social mobility. A diligent and fortunate farmer could acquire more land and eventually his descendants might become yangbans. The petty merchant could, by shrewd business practices and usury, acquire land and leisure for his son to study and raise the family status through success in the examinations. A yangban through profligacy or ill luck might lose much of his land holdings and drop back into the farmer class or live in genteel poverty. But the interlocking family system with sponging or helpful relatives, as the case might be, generally assured that the class status of the family was maintained.

The yangban class provided the officialdom. To the common people the government seemed remote and was represented more by the tax collector than the civil servant. Most public works such as road building and maintenance, construction of bridges, building of market places, and erection of public buildings were accomplished by cooperative efforts with some provincial or magisterial assistance. The army was usually weak. Its ill-trained soldiers, the second and third sons of poor families, occupied a very low rung on the social ladder.

From the court there spread down in the Confucian tradition a bureaucracy through the provinces and counties (or magistracies) to the towns. Villages were largely neglected except as a source of taxes and labor. In the village an unofficial type of democracy prevailed with local maintenance of law and order and with the carrying out of local public works. Contacts with town and county officials and adjudication of minor disputes or disruption of peace and order was the responsibility of the village elders, the male heads of the leading families. Usually on a rotating basis, one person was selected as the headman of the village.

The less contact with the government the better as far as the common people were concerned. The squabbles in the court and the jockeying for power by the high yangban families or cliques seemed to them a different world. Oppression of the common people was somewhat abated by the Confucian ethical system which curtailed the excesses and corruption of the bureaucrats. A wicked magistrate could be exposed by the traveling censor from the royal court, though this was a role enacted more often in stories and plays than in real life. One reason for the lack of effective action or strong position in the government on the part of the common people was that most of them had all they could do to wrest a living from the land. Rarely fortunate enough to have much formal education, they could communicate effectively with the government only through the yangbans. When drought or floods were very severe and economic hardships were unbearable the farm folk might explode into rebellions, but these were localized and were put down by magistrates and their hired "runners," or police.

Life of the Farmer

The farmers of the Korean peninsula have developed their agricultural practices through many centuries. The skills of the fathers have been passed on to the sons for generations. In modern Korea there are many of the characteristics of the past which are still an integral part of the agricultural scene: the large amount of human labor involved, the simple tools used, the emphasis upon cereal crops, especially the desired rice, the small and scattered plots operated as the family farm, and the dependence upon nature.

The average farm holdings are two or three acres per family. These holdings are in five or six scattered plots and often include both paddy fields for rice and upland fields for dry crops. Forest land may also be privately owned but more usually this is held communally by the village, clan or county. The small fields lie out a way from the village and the farmer going out to work them must walk, in extreme cases for as long as an hour, carrying his farm tools with him. The crops are commonly brought back to the farmstead for threshing or for drying in the sun.

The work is arduous for the land is not fertile and must have much care. In order to have good yields it is necessary to use fertilizer, either natural manure from the farmyard or in recent decades chemical fertilizer obtained from government sales offices. Fields are prepared for planting with an ox or cow and a simple wooden plow. Often the cow must be borrowed and is paid for by the donation of three or four times as long a period in human labor. Irrigation of the paddy fields depends largely upon rainfall, or simple catchment basins from which gravity ditches carry the water to the fields. In recent times, more elaborate irrigation systems have been developed which require donated labor in construction and regular payments for the water supplied. The dry fields are, of course, dependent solely upon rainfall and are not given such painstaking care as the paddy fields in plowing, harrowing, and weeding. On the dry fields barley, winter wheat, cotton, tobacco, millet, grain sorghum, beans and vegetables are grown, depending upon the climate. In southern Korea, where the growing season is long enough, barley may be planted as a seasonal crop on the drained paddy fields.

Some of the work is done communally by groups of farmers, often members of the same clan. This is particularly true in the heavy labor-demand periods of transplanting, weeding, and harvesting. At these times labor is exchanged, though occasionally farm laborers are hired from the poorest families in the village. Farm women, who devote most of their efforts to the raising of vegetables and the care of the home, work with the men in the fields at these times. It is an impressive sight to see fifteen or twenty people of both sexes and all ages standing ankle deep in the flooded paddy fields toiling at the backbreaking job of transplanting rice shoots in careful rows.

The cycle of the farm year and its associated festivals is based upon the lunar calendar in the old Korean tradition. The New Year season that falls in late January or early February is a particularly happy time. Farm work is at its lowest demand and the whole family takes off four or five days. Wearing new clothes they visit relatives and friends, have special meals, including rice and meat, and play games. In South Korea, on the fifteenth day of the first month, the boys

43

build bonfires and have fights with gangs of boys from neighboring villages for possession of these fires. On the fifth day of the fifth month, usually a warm spring day, the girls and young women have a special festival where they put up swings on poles or in tall trees. The prizes go to those that can swing the highest. On the fifteenth of the next month offerings are made to the gods of the fields beseeching bounteous harvests. On the fifteenth of the eighth month, the time of the full moon, there is the celebration of the Autumn Moon. At this time veneration is paid by food offerings at the graves to the ancestors of four generations and before. (The more recently deceased are honored by their direct families at various home ceremonies on the anniversaries of their death.) After these solemn ceremonies, the day is given over to games, dances, eating and drinking, culminating in moon-viewing parties to catch the first view of the full moon over the neighboring hills. If it arises in a propitious spot the village's crops will be good in the following year, and the first viewer will have specially good fortune. Bathing in the streams in the light of the autumn moon is said to ward off disease for the year. There are local and family festivals which are interspread with these lunar festivals. They play an important part in the life of the farmer, for they offer a needed break in the hard routine. The farmers' bands, the singing of both men's and women's groups, the bright clothes of the children, the decoration of the homes, the food and wine in relatively copious quantities, all bring gaiety to an otherwise drab and labor-filled existence.

This traditional way of life with all of its regional and local variations made a mosaic of folkways and loyalties which united the Korean people. Though there were differences between urban and rural folk, between life in the northern and southern part of Korea, between the pattern of society and economy on the plains and in the mountains, there was a totality—a Korean way of life. This traditional social pattern has been greatly transformed in recent decades under the impact of Japanese and Western forces. Some of the visible vestiges remain, however, and the present mores of the Koreans reflect much of their traditional past.

The Life of the Spirit

The Koreans are a volatile and emotional people, though naturally there are tremendous differences in temperament between individuals and it is difficult to generalize about them. Through the centuries the Koreans have had to look after their own family interests and accommodate themselves within each family so that they are shrewd and good-natured. They have pride in themselves and strong loyalties to their families. They resent slights from those outside their circle and often are inclined to argumentation and factionalism. They dislike being ordered about by others and many times appear lazy to those who expect them to do their bidding. Above all, they are resilient under hardship and expect to work hard at tasks they set for themselves.

As a people, the Koreans have lived close to their land. It is one of their most treasured of possessions. If it is their own, they use it with care and respect. If it is owned by a distant government or an absentee landlord, they no longer feel such concern. Their close ties with the land have led them to a reverence for nature, so that Korean religious life has strong undertones of nature worship. The Koreans, in following different religions, have found greatest appeal in those aspects which reflect a love of nature. Buddhist monasteries are situated in beautiful mountain valleys, graves of ancestors are located on hill slopes that look out over pleasant plains, Christian churches are built on hilltops. All Koreans are to a greater or lesser extent nature worshippers.

The oldest and most persistent religious beliefs of Korea

45

have been grouped together under the general term: Shamanism. This is a mingling of fear of evil spirits, veneration of good spirits, worship of natural phenomena, and belief in magical forces. Korean women will call upon *mudangs* or sorceresses to cleanse their homes of evil spirits or to pray for good fortune. There are few universal beliefs in Shamanism or any codification of religious laws. In fact some writers feel that using the term may be misleading, for it implies an organized religion rather than the elusive nature and spirit worship which is practiced in Korea.

The Koreans have a general belief in a divine being, but the strength of this belief depends upon the believer. The name for this central force, *Hananim,* was used by early Christian missionaries as the translation of the Christian word for God. This choice of words undoubtedly helped in the propagation of Christianity in Korea, for it enabled some synthesis to take place between the underlying religious ideas of the Koreans and the Christian views of a Universal Power. However, this widespread belief in a central divine destiny has not been a unifying force.

In contrast to the indefiniteness of Shamanism, Buddhism was much more highly organized in Korea. There have been numerous sects which held to strictly elaborated philosophical tenets. Temples were built, sometimes at great cost. Buddhism had its greatest power in the period of the Unified Silla dynasty (668–935) and of its successor, the Koryo dynasty (918–1392). Instead of remaining a strictly religious movement Buddhism became more and more a political and economic power in the Koryo period. Thus the reaction to its temporal power was severe in the Yi dynasty. During this period it became more and more decadent. Many of the monasteries were stripped of their excessive land holdings. Yet some, often depending upon the acumen and leadership of the individual abbots, managed to retain their influence. Pilgrimages were made to such monasteries for periods of meditation, among them were women desiring special divine favors. Common people often gathered at Buddhist temples for festive occasions and picnics. Some monasteries were controlled by families, for in some sects monks were not celibate. There was a great variation among the monasteries. Rites for the spirits of the dead were emphasized at some, at others time was largely devoted to serene contemplation, at still others elaborate rites marked by superstitious practices were carried on. In the last century there has been little dynamism in Korean Buddhism. In many cases there was a glorification of the dead past and little effort to meet the needs of the modern day.

Korean Confucianism developed more into an ethical system than a religion. The philosophical basis of Chu Hsi Confucianism was suited to the scholar who could read the classics and discuss with his fellow scholars fine distinctions in theories or write treatises of textual criticism. Confucian concepts of family relations, of "correctness" in personal relations, and of organization of government had a profound impact on the daily life of the people. Confucian phrases and precepts were used in the informal education within the Korean family by parents who could not read. The classics in simplified form were used in the village schools and children learned them by rote. The veneration of ancestors was carried out mainly under the Confucian concept of the family, but mixed with it were Shamanistic practices. In some cases this veneration became almost a religion, with the belief that the departed spirit would continue to care for the welfare of the family.

Traditionally many Koreans were eclectic in their religious practices. They combined their underlying belief in a central divine entity, *Hananim,* with a pervading worship of nature, and a fear or a veneration of natural objects which had evil or good associations in their minds. In case of trouble they would seek help from Buddhist monks and repeat prayers to Buddhist deities. Their family and social relations were guided by Confucian ethical systems.

When new religious concepts, such as Christianity or Chondogyo, a native religion, the Heavenly Way, made inroads in Korea toward the end of the nineteenth century, they met with little opposition from the mass of the Korean people, although the government opposed them, fearing the disruptive influence of new non-Confucian ideas. Throughout their history the Korean people, though deeply motivated in life and thinking by spiritual beliefs, have not had a strong national religion or religious base.

V. The Cultural Heritage of Korea

The Korean people have a deep respect for their cultural heritage and a veneration of the past which has given them solace in the present. It has also enabled them as a people to maintain a cultural entity when threatened by outside forces that sought to destroy or absorb them into their own cultures. At the same time they have assimilated numerous cultural expressions of other countries, particularly China. In recent times when vital new revolutionary forces have been active, great effort has been made to preserve the values of the past.

Throughout history there has been a major distinction between the culture of the small yangban class, the scholar-gentry group, and that of the common people. Yet in many aspects these two have merged. They both have had a profound love for the land and this is reflected in Korean culture. The scholars, enjoying leisure, were leaders in preserving and advancing Korean culture. Tending to be conservative, the yangbans helped greatly through their personal collections of art objects, through their studies of the classics, and through their individual creative efforts. The common people with their festivals and dances, their songs, proverbs, and sayings, contributed vibrancy and vitality. In recent times the oppression of outsiders, notably the Japanese, and the tumult of war have tended to bring the two groups together in their efforts to preserve and foster respect for the culture of the past.

Naturally, there have been changes in Korean culture, and a gradual fluctuation in style and in media of expression. Evelyn B. McCune described the nature of this development in *The Arts of Korea, An Illustrated History:* "The Koreans have been slow to change. This is an important clue to an understanding not only of their art but of their whole culture. It is not because they do not like novelties that they have been slow to change, but because they have been unwilling to relinquish the emotional satisfactions connected with their old arts until they are sure that the new will bring them equal comfort."

The affinity for natural phenomena that is shared by Koreans of every group can be seen in all their art forms. The most moving poems are odes to nature. Landscape painting is successful to the Korean when it stimulates a love of nature. Koreans use simple, natural materials. Rocks are shaped by sculpture into beauty of line and shape. Clay is formed by strength of expression and without complex decoration into beautiful cups and jars, utilitarian as well as beautiful.

The common people, whose life and well-being are so strongly tied to natural phenomena, have gone beyond mere appreciation of natural objects to a reverence for forces to which they attribute divine power. Thus they deify a tree, or a waterfall or a stone. They pay tribute to these divine forces in their songs and dances, in the choice of the location of homes and burial plots, and in their adherence to a cycle of living based upon the changing weather. The yangbans, whose life is more remote from nature and who are influenced by Confucian philosophical principles and rites, reveal a more sophisticated love of nature in their poetry, essays, painting and ceramics.

Architecture

Korean homes and buildings are traditionally made of native materials—rocks, wood, mud, and straw. They are located to take advantage of the warming sun or to be protected from the cold winds. In color and structure they appear to merge with the natural landscape. As Evelyn B. McCune has said: "Native Korean building has been well adjusted to the needs and tastes of the Korean people. It is suited to the rocky landscape and the temperate-zone climate; it is functional to a high degree and, though a branch of Chinese architecture in its general features, it has developed particular features of its own."

Chinese architecture used three of the main basic building techniques, the post-and-lintel, arch-and-vault, and cantilever construction. The fourth, the truss, was not used and, as a consequence, the roofs resting on the post-and-lintel were complex and heavy. Korean architecture made local adaptations to the Chinese architectural designs, using local materials—notably wood and stone. Korea has an abundance of granite and this is a basic construction material. Korean woods are mostly soft, so that they must be renewed or protected. Differences in detail developed, for example in the designs pressed into the bricks and tiles. Little color is used for decoration; the natural grain of the wood or the simple color and soft texture of the oiled paper used on the floor give beauty to the buildings. Because of the mountainous terrain Korean buildings are not arranged with strict symmetry as in the Chinese style, though as in China there has been emphasis upon town and city planning. In Korea this planning has been more devoted to accommodating the houses to the terrain and, in particular, opening them out to a distant view.

51

A particular form of architecture of persisting importance has been the tombs. Some of the early forms are the step-pyramids, roughly half the size of those in the Nile valley, built in the Yalu valley during the Koguryo period (37 B.C.–668 A.D.). Other stone tombs were built in this period near the present city of Pyongyang. Some of these are distinctive for their square design and for their wall murals. These paintings depict dragons, warriors, and court ladies; the most famous is of a tortoise and a snake entwined in a creation symbol. The tombs of the period of the Three Kingdoms and of succeeding periods, even to the present, were built in beautiful scenic spots.

Another form of architecture which has been preserved from these early days is the fortress cities. The mountain peaks were used as a part of the fortifications and along the crests were built crenulated stone walls pierced by gates. During times of invasion, fortress cities tucked back in the hills provided places of refuge. This system of defense was continued into quite modern times and the remnants of the stone walls may be seen, for example, around Seoul and other cities. Cities of this sort were often irregular in shape, for the walls followed the summit of the hills.

Buddhist temples, though often copied from Chinese prototypes, nevertheless had distinctive Korean features. Their location and the view they commanded were of prime importance. Associated with the Buddhist temples were stone pagodas of various design. One of the most famous temples of Korean design is the Horyuji temple built near Nara in Japan. Here the Buddhist art of the Paekche period (18 B.C.–663 A.D.) has been preserved, for Paekche was a cultural bridge to Japan from China, India, and Persia. Buddhist temples of Silla and Koryo times still remain in remote mountain valleys of Korea. Built to appear detached from the world, they were places of striking beauty. Except for their heavy tile roofs, they were of relatively simple design. The eaves and the pillars may have been decorated, but the strength of the pillars showed through in the natural grain of the wood.

The palaces of Korea also reflect the Chinese influence, especially those of the Yi dynasty in Seoul. They were built about courtyards with separate pavilions where ponds, trees, and flowering plants gave added detail and beauty. In these, too, the Koreans made their own adaptations. Most marked was a deviation from regularity and symmetry to fit the natural terrain. A great wealth of decoration covered the pillars and the fitted roof beams of the palaces. These designs were usually symbolic: animals, some of mythical beasts or birds; floral decorations, including the lotus which was a Buddhist symbol from India; and geometric designs, for example the ancient swastika, were common decorative themes. Some of these designs were also used in the Confucian shrines or memorial buildings for famous personages, which dotted the Korean countryside.

Sculpture

Buddhist influence on the culture of Korea was very strong. Some of its greatest art treasures were designed for the veneration of the Buddha. However, Korean sculpture was not solely Buddhist in nature. For example, the dolmens, rock structures similar to those found elsewhere in the world, though not in China and Japan, indicate the Central Asian influence on the Korean people. The dolmens, commonly four standing rocks about the height of a man, capped with a fifth rock slab, are found in plains in North and South Korea. Among the conjectures for their use are that they mark burial places of chieftains or were used for a form of sun worship. Whatever their origin, they are impressive reminders of the past.

Buddhist art flourished especially in the period of the Three Kingdoms, in the succeeding unified Silla period (668–935), and the following Koryo period (919–1392). It was at its height in Paekche, the third kingdom in the southwest of Korea. Though the temples and the sculpture made of wood have long since been destroyed, some of the brick and stone pagodas still stand. The best illustrations of Buddhist sculpture by Paekche artists are now found in Japan because some of them fled there at the breakup of the kingdom.

One of the most impressive examples of Buddhist statuary of the Silla dynasty was hewn in natural rock at Sokkuram, a cave high on a hill crest looking out over the sea, near the city of Kyongju in southeastern Korea. A number of figures were carved in relief around the walls. The central figure, an eleven-foot, solid granite, seated Buddha symbolizes tranquillity and peace, eternally on watch. The statue, in the words of Evelyn B. McCune, "is rendered in almost stark simplicity. Its garment is merely indicated by shallow cuttings; its conventional sacred marks, such as the topknot and the spot between the eyes, are present but inconspicuous. . . . (The figure) is especially pleasing to Korean worshippers, who see in it a pledge that the Buddha will protect them against any invasion from across the eastern sea. The aloof, yet listening, pose of the Sokkuram Buddha has had, and still has, a tremendous appeal to countless Korean worshippers. . . . The style of the sculpture is clearly that of Tang China, but many of the features—the ambulatory arrangement of the chapel, the orderly disposition of the various figures, their proportions, their austerity, the contrast of the strongly individual and particularized earthly figures with the ethereal and generalized divine and semidivine figures—are wholly unique. This shrine is certainly one of the treasures of the ancient Orient."

There are countless other Buddhist sculptures of these olden times to be found in Korea. Some are rather crude stone figures, others are large wooden and gilded statues,

54

still others are delicate, filigreed little figures of gold or gold gilding over wood or bronze. Many of them have a distinctive Korean style which is simplified rather than garish and stresses form and shape. Buddhist pagodas are also common. Some of them are simple, of five or seven stories, and without much decoration; others have bas-reliefs of Buddhist figures or symbols on their side panels. Large bells are hung at the temples to call the worshippers and to be used in religious ceremonies. Many of these by their shape and decoration were works of art.

Sculptured figures of scholars and animals often guard the tombs of kings and yangbans. More primitive types of these protective figures were erected by the common people at the entrance to their villages. These simple carved wooden "devil posts," as they were called by Western missionaries, had color and vitality, despite their crude design. Then there were memorial tablets carved in stone, often beautiful for the calligraphy on them and for the floral or geometric decorations of their bases.

Pottery

While sculpture as an art form declined in artistic merit, another form of art—pottery—flourished in the Koryo period (918–1392 A.D.). Actually there was an ancient tradition of pottery making in Korea. In Neolithic times pottery was made with distinctive comb-markings, or parallel wavy lines, similar to that found in Siberia and northern Europe. These have been found in the valleys and along the shores of Korea. In the hilly regions of the interior another type of undecorated early pottery has been found. Evelyn B. McCune writes: "The Korean peninsula is rich in ceramic clays, every province having pits. Pottery, therefore, was not only an early culture-product but has continued to the present day to be a major one. It has been produced throughout the country for the daily use and enjoyment of every class of society and for all levels of sophistication and income. The ceramic industry can therefore be looked upon as one measuring stick by which to appraise the prosperity or decline of Korean economic conditions throughout the history of the country." There has long been a tradition of making simple articles for daily use in homes. These are red or black, made from soft paste and hand potted. The simple lines, for example of the water and pickle jars, are attractive, though the jars can scarcely be considered works of art.

At the start of the Koryo period the artisans began to use a new type of clay product, "the gray hard-paste that was produced on the potter's wheel and was decorated and glazed . . . (in the) famous colors and patterns that distinguish Koryo ware from all others." The original technique was derived from the potters in the Shantung peninsula of China. However, it was not long before the Koryo potters developed advanced techniques of their own, using typical Korean shapes, glazes and decorations. Noteworthy were the delicate grey-green celadons and inlaid ware. Many types of designs were incised into the clay base before it was glazed. Among other methods was "the inlaid celadon, a technique which was a Korean specialty. By this method an intaglio design, made by hand or mold, was filled flush with the body of the piece by threads of black or white clay, sometimes enhanced by spots of red. The inlay (*saggom* in Korean) was then inserted, the piece was baked again. The invention of this technique is thought by some to have been the work of a single master potter." Mrs. McCune further notes: "Another original contribution of the Korean potter was his use of underglaze copper oxide, which turned a brilliant red when baked. This was a Korean discovery of great significance for the later pottery of the whole Far East."

One of the reasons contributing to the fame of the Koryo

ware has been the comparatively great abundance of it remaining in modern times. Many thousands of objects were buried in tombs according to the customs of the period. They have recently been recovered in excellent condition and display in striking fashion this lost art in many of the museums of the world. Partly due to the Mongol invasions of the thirteenth century and partly because of the generally little value that was placed upon it, "the whole class of celadon pottery, died out altogether and, with it, the secret of the lustrous range of blue-green glazes."

During the Yi dynasty there continued to be manufactured large amounts of common ceramic clay products but the pottery declined in artistic merit. Blues and greyish whites were used and "bold and splashy" decorations; also some new techniques of incising and stamping were introduced.

Painting

Just as Koryo pottery was initially derived from China, so painting in its early forms in Korea was adopted from the techniques developed by scholar-artists of China. Painting has been a classic art in Korea. The earliest examples which have been preserved are the murals on the tombs of the Three Kingdoms and the Lolang colony. It was, however, not until the early Yi dynasty (1392–1910) that painting became a major art form. Silk, paper and brushes suitable for water colors had been perfected by this time. Chinese influence was strong, but the Korean artists with their love of nature and of land emphasized natural subjects—birds, flowers, bamboo— and landscapes, particularly combining mountains and water. The styles that landscape painters initially followed were developed in southern China.

Over the centuries there gradually developed more and more of a distinctive Korean style. There were two types of painters—the yangbans or members of the court who had the leisure to become skilled amateur painters, and the professional painters of high talent and little wealth who were supported by the court or wealthy patrons. Some painters were more intuitive in their painting, bringing in hidden meanings often related to Son (Zen in Japanese) Buddhist thought. One of the most famous of the early Yi dynasty professional painters was An Kyon (Kyondongja, 1400–1470). He was especially known for his landscapes. Evelyn B. McCune quotes a description of a segment of one of his paintings that was written a hundred years later by a Korean scholar: "The cottage and trees in front of the mountain are as calm as if they were sleeping, and the brushwood gate is open. An aged man who went to the market to sell his wares is on the way back, and a boy is spreading his net upon the sands. The mountains slope gently; they seem to sheathe a mighty sword. The vast expanse of sea and sky join in the distance . . . in a bamboo thicket . . . there is an empty cottage. Who is to retire from the world to live here?"

One of the most famous painters of the next century was Lady Sin (Sa Imdong, 1512–1599). The second daughter of an impoverished scholar, she learned the classics as well as the art of painting which she began at the age of seven. She became famed, also, as the mother of a scholar-statesman (Yi I, or Yulgok). A painter of simplicity and clarity, she came to be favorably compared with An Kyon, despite the fact that she was a woman. Mrs. McCune gives this characterization of her: "The conservative nature of Madame Sin's academic training was apparent in her devotion to tradition . . . along with her reverence for tradition, however, was a pronounced drive to break with tradition, to establish her own style and repertoire out of the facts of her everyday Korean experience, and it is this which endeared her to her countrymen as much as anything else. . . . Madame Sin's prestige rested first upon her success in her family life—the plain living and high thinking which was, and still is, the Korean ideal though it is only too often neglected by the official class—and second, upon her very substantial success as a gifted and sensitive artist."

Another artist of great repute, Yi Chong (Tanun, born in 1541), suffered the loss of his right arm during the wars against the Japanese (1592–1598), but gained even greater skill with his left hand. He was especially noted for his paintings of bamboo. As Mrs. McCune notes: "He liked to paint bamboo because he admired its qualities; it always grew straight and was never crooked; it was inflexible, stiff and unyielding, but at the same time it was graceful and was thus associated with the supreme Confucian virtues of loyalty, integrity, and sweet reasonableness."

These are only three of the many artists who were painting in Korea during the early Yi dynasty. In the seventeenth century there were even more painters, but many of them followed existing patterns of Korean and Chinese painting. A few continued in original styles and received inspiration not only from China but from Japan where color prints began to flourish as a form of popular art. Some of them such as Kim Myongguk (Yondam), who was active in 1623–1650, gave verve and humor to some of his paintings, though Yondam could be meticulous in his landscape paintings if he wished to be so.

During the eighteenth century Korean art began to break away from Chinese patterns and became more distinctive. In the words of Mrs. McCune: "At almost all previous periods, the country had been inundated by the finished products of a discouragingly superior civilization. During the eighteenth century, in isolation, Korean art was freed to some extent to concentrate on the development of local ideas. . . . Old forms remained in use, since they contained all the symbols that were needed by the Korean for the expression of their most complex, profound, and even contradictory feelings." One of the artists, Chang Son (Kyomjae, 1676–1709), "by means of the simple expedient of basing landscapes upon actual Korean scenes and Korean subjects, did a great deal toward changing painting in Korea from a transplantation to a home-grown product. Painting took on a new life. It became lively and comprehensible and was nourished by the springs of Korean culture itself." Chang Son during his long life had a number of students who continued his practice of painting from nature and life. Some of these artists specialized in subjects such as horses, plum blossoms, cats, fish, and so on. All of them were realistic in their painting, suggesting natural objects and people often with only a few brush lines. There was an increasing influence of Western art and some experimenting with new perspectives.

Calligraphy

Just as in painting so in calligraphy there was for centuries an imitation of Chinese styles. As these styles changed in China, Korean calligraphers followed the new trends, particularly those of the free-flowing Sung dynasty styles. Kim Chonghui (Wondaung, 1786–1856) developed a distinctive style, known by another of his pen names, Chusa. As a young man, he had studied in Peking. He was thoroughly grounded in the classical Chinese forms and wrote essays and guides for students of calligraphy. When his family was involved in court intrigues and he was banished from the court, first to Chju Island and then to north Korea, students and scholars flocked after him to study the semicursive Chusa style and receive critiques of their works.

Poetry

The scholar in traditional Korean life was not only a painter and a calligrapher but also a poet. This was a form of expression which could combine painting and literature.

Through the centuries Koreans have appreciated poetic expression. Many Koreans memorize well-known poems and give great respect to the person who can evoke emotions through the brevity of a poem. In addition, Korean poetry has been closely associated with music and the dance.

Among the scholars were some who were profound students and lovers of Chinese civilization and culture. These persons wrote in classical Chinese and a few became well-known among Chinese scholars of their day. Just as did the painters, they tended increasingly to use Korean themes and backgrounds for their poetry. However, they were generally bound by the Chinese forms of poetry so that though Korean in subject matter, their poetry was not quite indigenous to Korea.

The earliest purely Korean poetry were songs which were sung at religious festivals when the gods of heaven were propitiated for good harvests in the spring and which rendered thanks in the fall for their bounty. These were passed down by word of mouth. The verses were usually short, with a refrain which could be sung by large groups. In the period of the Three Kingdoms poetry came to be more related to events of daily life, though there was still some religious poetry, often devoted to veneration of the Buddha. A few of the poems of Silla have been preserved. During this period the poets became increasingly sophisticated. A formal structure was developed starting with a main theme, elaborating on the theme and concluding with a short epigram. During the Koryo period which followed there was a growth in the use of Chinese forms of poetry. Long narrative poems were sung which had within them a refrain which could be repeated by the group of listeners. These poems were on themes such as love, nature, famous places and historical events.

At the start of the Yi dynasty (1392–1910) a new form of Korean poetry flowered. This was the *sijo,* a short poem of three lines. Many sijo were composed on the spur of the moment, others were more carefully written. The most famous have been repeated over the centuries and over 2,000 have been preserved in anthologies. The form of the sijo was determined by the nature of the Korean language. The character of the poem matched the Korean love of epigrammatic expression. Usually the sijo began with an apt descriptive phrase setting the theme or asking a question, followed by an elaboration, suggestive of the theme. It ended with a turn of thought or conclusion drawn from the theme.

The common emotions; love, loyalty, love of nature, and lament were depicted in these short poems. The sijo were often written to commemorate times of celebration or anniversaries. The sijo of Hwang Chini (1506–1544) are well-known, though few in number. A *kisang,* or professional dancer and singer, she was the daughter of a scholarly family. She used natural subjects—rain, wind, the moon, mountains, streams—and enhanced them with subtle meanings. Another famous poet was Yun Sundo (Kosan, 1587–1671). He had a political career often marked by exile for his forthright expression of opinion. For a time he was tutor to the son of the King. His best sijo written in his scholarly retreats are reflective poems depicting nature. Particularly famous is his series on fishing, the Angler's Calendar. One of his poems which is a personal favorite of the author and which was translated by a Korean friend is:

"Morning mists lift in the river valley,
The sun's soft rays peep over the hills.
Creak, creak, sound the boatman's oars.
Beautiful are the scenes of the village by the stream,
Even lovelier are the views of distant landscapes."

The common people not only repeated sijo written by the yangbans and kisangs but composed and recited their own, usually with less strict attention to the rules of composition. Another form of poetry developed during the Yi dynasty were long poems, almost like prose, that were often descriptions of places visited or of social customs observed. These were more restricted to the scholarly class; the common people could not memorize them easily as they did some of the sijo.

Music

The Koreans are great lovers of music. For example, in modern Christian churches choirs are equalled in their contribution to the religious service by the fervent and inspired congregational singing, which is not often the case in American churches. Koreans seem to have a natural ability to sing and do so on all occasions. The sound of flutes often breaks the still of the night. A constantly repeated chant lends rhythm to the raising and pulling of a heavy load. Drums provide a rhythm for the transplanting of rice. Music pervades their lives.

This love of music goes far back in the past. Ancient Chinese records speak of Korea as "the land where the people love singing." The earliest songs were those associated with the festivals to honor the spirits of the planting and of the harvest. It was natural that music would accompany the dances and that the words sung were poems. From these early times songs were composed and handed down to accompany all sorts of common tasks, such as plowing fields, transplanting rice, sowing barley, hauling in fish nets, sawing wood, lulling children, winding thread, weaving cloth, and carrying heavy loads. The accompaniment for such songs were made by hand clapping or drumming on resonant objects. From such folk music more formal instruments and melodies were developed.

China exerted a great influence on Korean music also. This was particularly true of the highly stylized court music which

63

first developed in the Silla period. At that time a school was formed to train musicians. Chinese musical instruments were imported; some of them continued in use in Korea after becoming obsolete in China. Among the Korean instruments of ancient, as well as modern, usage were two long zithers, one of six strings which was struck by a piece of bamboo and the other of twelve strings which was plucked with the fingers. Flutes of various kinds have also been locally developed. The scales for the court music generally followed the Chinese tonal system, though there were some Korean adaptations. The regular rhythm in some Chinese styles which used one note to a syllable, was changed in Korea to a rhythm with notes of varied duration. These rhythms were very slow and stately in court music, much more rapid in common music and with abrupt endings.

Korean court music became even more stylized in the Koryo period. More complicated types of instruments were used: sundial-shaped drums, round drums, cylindrical oboes and chimes made of metal slabs of varied length and thickness. In the early Yi dynasty there was a continuation of this Chinese-inspired, Korean-adapted music. Even the kings composed music, one helping to develop a better system of musical notation. Along with the improvement of ritualistic court music, music among the common people flourished, though they had less formal and elaborate instruments. Singing with the accompaniment of flutes, horns and drums was common in the rural areas. In the cities and among the yangbans, the singers were often trained kisangs, or dancing girls, who were accompanied by zithers and drums. Poems were set to music, usually to Korean rhythms.

The folk songs of the people have been handed down for generations. They often have local connotations and are associated with the different provinces of Korea. One of the most famous is *Arirang*. This was a basic refrain with countless verses, many of them composed on the spur of the moment to suit a particular occasion or mood. The refrain which repeats the word arirang refers to a mountain pass. By extension this word also connotes mankind's journey through time. A rough translation of the refrain is:

"Arirang, Arirang, O Arirang,
The pass of Arirang is long and arduous."

The verses which then follow, interspersed by the refrain, vary from the sublime to the ridiculous, from the haunting to the salacious. A few that the author remembers well may be translated roughly as:

"The pass of Arirang is a most unique one,
As I trudge up and up, tears come to my eyes."

Refrain

"In the front of the house the young scholar is late at his books,
In the rear of the house his neglected bride is weeping."

Refrain

"The times in which we live are most trying,
To this thousand miles of rivers and mountains
may peace and prosperity come."

Dance

The earliest dances in Korea were performed as a part of religious ceremonies. They were related to the festivals of the gods of the harvest. Old tomb paintings depict the verve and grace of movement of some of these dances. Dancing has always been a group activity in Korea with musical accompaniment and with audience participation. For some of the dances masks were worn; the costumes were usually brilliantly colorful.

The dances of Korea have had a long history. During the period of the Three Kingdoms, dances were introduced from China, some even from Turkestan. In the Koryo dynasty, formalized dance forms were brought from China, some of them for Confucian ceremonies, and colorful and varied dances were included as a part of Buddhist festivals. In the Yi dynasty the court sponsored formal dances with set patterns. These were performed at functions such as the visits of envoys from China and staged as colorful spectaculars. A book published in 1494 gives a full account of fifteen dances, eight from China and seven from Korea, describing in detail the music and costumes. New dances were developed, including some by the kings themselves. Women were the dancers at the court and from this background there developed the kisangs who entertained at formal banquets, ladies who could dance, sing, play musical instruments and recite and compose poems.

Besides the religious and court dances, there were folk dances which, in contrast, had much more freedom of expression and much more improvisation. They combined dance and music with much livelier participation by dancers and audience. Costumes were simpler, often only a colorful sash worn over regular clothes or strips of paper or cloth attached to a headpiece which whirled out as the dancer turned his head. Simulated swords were used in some dances with great dexterity. Drums, sometimes carried by the dancers themselves, provided the common accompaniment. Some of the local dances included the use of masks which were village property handed down over the centuries.

Drama

Some of the early Korean dances were forms of drama, telling stories through motion and song. Thus drama and dance were developed together in traditional Korean culture. They were particularly enjoyed by the common people; drama did not truly develop in the courts, but in the villages. The drama often used masks, particularly for the disguise of humans as animals or as divine beings. From this use of masks the puppet plays may have developed. These were popular in the rural areas; a corner of the market place was often used for such plays. The enduring themes of the puppet plays and the dramas were attractive to the common people: the downfall of an apostate Buddhist monk or a rapacious yangban, the triumph of an impoverished, honest scholar or a kisang of humble origin, the loyalty of a wife in conflict with a scheming concubine. Often there was satire of the ruling classes.

One of the most famous stories of Korea was the romance of *Chun-hyang*, sometimes translated as "Fragrance of Spring." The story was read as a novel or put into dramatic form as a play. Its exact origin some 250 years ago is not known. Its writer, who set in prose the story which had been told as a folk tale for centuries, was probably a scholar who did not want his name associated with the story. It went through many versions, including some set to music, and had numerous additions and deletions. The plot in brief is the love story of a boy of the yangban class and a girl, Chun-hyang, the daughter of a kisang. The boy goes off to Seoul to study and take his civil service examinations. The girl becomes a kisang. Years later the boy, now a traveling censor for the court in Seoul, comes to the rural county to investigate the evil doings of the local magistrate. The girl, on the point of being forced to become the mistress of the magistrate, is saved from this fate by the boy who strips the magistrate of his office. They marry despite their different origins and live happily ever after. Koreans love to see this drama and appreciate many of the songs and stories which embroider the plot. The earthy humor added by the exploits of the servant of the yangban is greatly enjoyed.

67

Prose

As can be seen from the illustration of the "Fragrance of Spring," novels and drama may be closely related in Korea. Close, also, is the relation between novels and poetry. The Chinese influence has been strong throughout Korean literary history. Some of the Korean novels were modeled on popular Chinese books. In some cases, Korean writers set their novels in China of past times in order to escape political retaliation, though the stories were obviously applicable to the Korean scene. In addition to novels, Koreans wrote essays and short stories in the manner of the Chinese literati. One of them, for example, Choe Chi-won passed the literary examinations in China in 885 and was recognized as a noted scholar and writer by the Chinese.

The earliest literature of Korea was based upon the oral tradition of story tales, songs and religious ceremonies. Much of the early writing was done in classical Chinese, or by taking Chinese characters for Korean sounds. Some of the earliest Korean literature was the compilation by court officials of histories of previous kingdoms. Notable were the *Samguk sagi* ("Historical Record of the Three Kingdoms," compiled by Kim Pusik in 1145), and the *Samguk yusa* ("Remains of the Three Kingdoms," compiled in 1284 by a Buddhist monk, Iryon). In these, folk tales and a few poems of the past kingdoms were written down. Later, works were written which helped to preserve the traditions of the Korean people. Some of these books told tales vividly of supernatural beings or gave human attributes to animals or flowers. Often the stories satirized the Buddhist monks or the yangbans. Court diaries and fictionalized accounts of historical events, particularly the overcoming of Japanese raiders, were popular.

One of the famous novels is the *Cloud Dream of the Nine,* written by Kim Manjung in 1687 for his mother. This went through numerous editions. (It was translated into English by James S. Gale in 1922.) The story is set in Tang China, though patently Korean in background. It has many Buddhist allusions with Confucian and some Taoist ideas also incorporated. The story relates how the hero meets each of nine girls and makes them his wives or concubines.

During the Yi dynasty Korean literature developed in new ways. The invention of the Korean alphabet opened up a wide audience of readers, especially for stories to be read by women and the increasingly important middle classes. At the same time, with the growth of neo-Confucian thought, and with the emphasis upon the Civil Service examination system based on Confucian classics, there was a great flowering of scholarly writing, in particular historical writing and essays on literary subjects. The Confucian classics were analyzed in depth. Often essays were moralistic, with emphasis upon rites and correct behavior in the Confucian pattern. As time went on there was more divergence between the literature for the common people and the scholarly works, often written in classical Chinese.

Some essayists turned from the ancient themes and wrote on practical issues such as land reform and governmental reorganization. They were influenced by new ideas derived from China. Often they were members of embassies sent to Peking who had cultural contacts with Chinese and Catholic scholars. Included among their works were essays on Catholic religious thought and on scientific ideas from the West. These writers also departed from classical Chinese and used more modern Chinese or Korean for their writing. As the Confucian writing became more sterile in ideas and more remote from the realities of Korea, the authors, who had derived new ideas from China and the West and applied these to the Korean situations, became more popular.

The output of fiction written in the Korean language increased greatly. There was demand for such writing among the growing middle classes as well as among the yangbans and their ladies. Earlier novels were greatly influenced in their form and plot by Chinese exemplars, but increasingly they became devoted to the Korean economic and social scene which was undergoing change. An interesting feature of some of these novels was the device of taking the hero on travels throughout the eight provinces of Korea. This widened the horizons of the readers and helped to change the strictly provincial loyalty to one of a more national scope. Many of these novels were historical romances developing a basis for pride in Korean heroes, particularly those who fought against the Japanese. They spoke out against class distinctions and were opposed to the rigidities of Confucian doctrines and to the excesses of Buddhist monks and abbots. Characters such as the virtuous wife and the honest kisang, or the tyrannical mother-in-law and the scheming concubine, appealed to the women readers. "The Cloud Dream of the Nine" and the "Fragrance of Spring" already noted were examples of this popular fiction which condemned vice and lauded virtue.

Folk Tales and Proverbs

The common people of Korea through the centuries have not been great readers. It was not until the Yi dynasty that a simple alphabet was invented, but even then it did not have great usage among them, for the yangbans thought of it as too common and so not a great amount was written in it. Thus, the bulk of the people continued their oral tradition rather than a written one. This resulted in, however, a richness of story telling. The grandfathers and grandmothers, as well as the itinerant storyteller, kept this tradition alive. Children grew to love these stories which often had simple moral maxims. A favorite character was a *tokgabi,* a mischievous gremlin. For example, to deal with a tokgabi one was told never to look up at it with fear because then it would grow larger and larger, but always to look down on it steadfastly for then it would become smaller and smaller and disappear. This was, by extension, useful advice to youngsters beset with fears of the unknown.

Many stories were humorous. The author remembers from his childhood one about a farmer who had gone to the market town and joined in a tug-of-war. His team celebrated their victory with much rice wine. On the way home he wandered off the path and fell asleep. During the night a tiger came and sniffed at him. In his dreams the farmer thought he was at the tug-of-war again and, grabbing the tiger's tail and pulling with all his strength, yelled mightily the Korean version of "Heave-ho!" The tiger, terrified, finally succeeded in pulling away. When the farmer awoke in the sober dawn he was amazed to find tiger hairs on the palms of his hands, then vaguely recalled his dream. He walked on and came to his village to find the people were organizing a hunt for a tiger which had carried off a baby during the night. He joined the hunt and after awhile saw the tiger on a hill crest. "Wait a moment," he said, and with all of his might yelled "Heave-ho!" The villagers could scarcely believe their eyes as they watched the tiger drop the baby and flee in terror. The farmer became the hero of the village and lived the rest of his happy life as "the brave man who scares tigers."

Korean proverbs and pithy sayings were well-known and much used by the common people of Korea. Some of them are universal in their applicability, such as the following:

"Making a beginning is half the job."
"Another man's cake always look larger than one's own."
"As silly as slapping one's own cheek."
"An empty cart rattles the loudest."
"There is no sense in pouring knowledge into a pig's ear."
"Tap even a stone bridge before crossing it."

KOREA

"Too often people repair a barn after the cow has been
stolen."
"One eye finds more truth than two ears."

Sports and Games

The common people of Korea have been hard working because of the poverty of their land, but they have also liked to
play hard when the opportunity arose. Thus many of their
games were rough or required much endurance. In contrast,
the yangbans adopted many quiet games from China, such as
forms of chess or checkers. They loved to fish in a quiet stream
or sit admiring a peaceful view.

Children's games were common to both groups. A form of
hopscotch or rope jumping could be played on a dusty roadway or courtyard. A favorite boy's game was to hit a stick in
the air and then hit it with another stick. He who hit it the
farthest was the winner. Another game used a shuttlecock
made of a couple of metal coins and some chicken feathers;
it had to be kept in the air as long as possible by kicking it
aloft on the instep. Girls liked to seesaw by jumping on a
board and sending the partner opposite high in the air, her
pigtails flying even higher. In the spring girls and young
women loved to swing way out over the landscape on swings
made with thick straw ropes tied to a strong horizontal branch
of a tall pine. Prizes would be given to the one who could
swing the highest.

Some of the sports of the yangbans such as archery were derived from the military tradition. This became very formalized with elaborate shooting galleries erected across a ravine
from the targets. Perhaps from the same tradition was a dangerous sport of the common people, rock throwing, where
one village contested with another on a common ground between them. Another inter-village contest was a tug-of-war

72

with a heavy straw rope. Kite flying was a sport of all boys and young men. Sometimes contests were held in which the strings of the kites were crossed high in the air and then through sawing of the strings the loser's kite string was broken and it sailed away. Korean men had wrestling contests, particularly at the market days. The wrestlers would each grasp the cloth belt worn by the other then attempt to trip his opponent by kicking his feet out from under him. The prize for the winner who had vanquished all challengers would be a bull or a calf. This is similar to the Japanese *judo;* the Koreans also have their own versions of *karate* and *jujitsu.*

VI. Japan's Modernizing of Korea

In 1876 the doors of the Hermit Nation were forced open by Japan. For the following seventy years it was aggressive Japan, emerging as a modern industrial nation relatively strong in military power, that dominated Korea. Japan's Korea policy fluctuated during the decades, reflecting her own domestic trends. As one of Korea's closest neighbors, Japan today still continues to play a significant role. However, Koreans have bitter memories of their days as an object of Japanese expansion and, after 1910, as a colony of Japan, so that genuine Korean-Japanese cooperation is strongly opposed. To outsiders, new to the scene, this lack of economic and social relations of two close neighbors seems unwarranted. But the events of the seventy years are not easily erased from the minds of the Koreans and they must be understood.

The Loss of Korean Independence

Korea, though it attempted isolation, was not unaware of the outside world prior to 1876. There was an infiltration of

74

Western ideas by way of China. Korean scholars on tribute or study missions to China brought back Chinese translations of Western books. Contacts were made in Peking with Jesuits and other Western scholars. The conservative Korean court was violently opposed to this "new learning" and suppressed such non-Confucian ideas. Christian missionaries, Catholic and Protestant, attempted with limited success to smuggle their way into Korea. Some of them became martyrs for their faith upon being discovered on Korean soil. However, the ferment in China caused by the impact of the West did spread over into Korea. It is interesting to speculate what might have been the fate of Korea if it had adopted the new ways at that time. But the faction-ridden court, the estrangement of the landlord-scholar class from the common people, and the geographic separations within Korea made impossible any true liberalization of the political and economic life of Korea and any unification of purpose. A misguided veneration for and trust in Imperial China still existed.

Western nations attempted to open Korea during the 1800's. Survey ships cruised the coasts. Adventurers tried to penetrate inland, some on such peculiar expeditions as seeking to rob royal graves of their supposed treasures of gold and the bones of royal ancestors which could be held for ransom. Military forces, the French in 1866 and the Americans in 1871, made landings and fought skirmishes, but these served only to frighten the Koreans and harden their desire for isolation. The court was under the control of a regent, the Taewongun. He was in fact the natural father of the King, for the King had been adopted by his uncle, the previous monarch who had been childless. This autocratic regent was strongly opposed to non-Chinese intervention in Korea. He particularly distrusted the Japanese and the Christian missionaries who were clamoring for entrance into the Hermit Nation.

Finally in 1876 the Japanese, who had had limited dealings

with Korea for decades at trading posts near Pusan, forced the Korean court to sign a modern treaty. This action was approved by China. Quickly, the Western nations followed. The American-Korean treaty of friendship was signed in 1882. In this treaty there were the usual phrases of the treaties of this nature: each signator would exert its good offices, in case other powers dealt unjustly or oppressively with either government. Years later the Korean royal court attempted, through an American friendly to the royal family, to appeal to the United States for assistance on the basis of this treaty, but this was abortive.

The Japanese in their desire to gain advantages in Korea and to force reforms within Korea had some important rivals. In the Korean court conservative pro-Chinese factions opposed them. A key figure was the Queen, a member of the powerful Min clan. Though an attempt to assasinate her was unsuccessful in a palace revolt in 1882, late in 1895 she was murdered in an attack on the palace by a gang of Japanese ruffians supposedly bent on protecting the court.

Another source of Korean opposition was a rebellious group with a strong rural base, the Tonghak. These were mainly followers of an indigenous religious movement, the Chundogyo, or the Heavenly Way. This group proclaimed a doctrine appealing to the Koreans with its promise of immediate heavenly rewards on earth. It was opposed to foreign religions, particularly Christianity. The uprisings resulted in an appeal by the frightened Korean court for Chinese troops. However, the Japanese, not to be outdone, intervened. Actually, the rebellion was put down by Korean troops; even so the Japanese sent in troops, to the embarrassment of their own diplomatic officers. This action, moreover, had the serious consequence of being one factor leading to the Sino-Japanese war of 1894–1895, in which the Japanese soundly defeated the ill-equipped and ill-led Chinese. One result of the war was that China formally recognized the independence of Korea.

Foreign powers—the Russians, French, British and Americans—began to show concern over the rise of Japanese power in Korea and elsewhere. The Russians with their short border on Korea and their desires for economic control in neighboring Manchuria began to emerge as a powerful force. The Korean King, frightened by the pressure of the Japanese, fled on February 11, 1896, to the Russian consulate. From this haven he reorganized the government. A year later the King moved to a newly constructed Western-style palace, an architectural monstrosity. Unfortunately in some respects, the new cabinet was conservative and based on cliques rather than national loyalties. A liberal-nationalistic group, the Independence Club, headed by an American-trained Korean tried to excite the people to reform and to influence the court. The Club was not successful and was virtually disbanded in 1898. The inefficient and corrupt Korean court continued to be estranged from the common people and made only feeble efforts to develop military power and institute a modern educational system.

The Japanese, after their setback, continued to be concerned in Korean affairs. They negotiated agreements with the Russians and opened their doors to Korean students. They discussed with the Russians, near the turn of the century, the idea of separating Korea into two zones of influence separated by the 38th parallel, and later into three zones with a neutral area between the 37th and 39th parallels. The Russians had obtained valuable timber concessions in northern Korea. Western business men, including Americans, obtained concessions for gold mining and for railroad construction.

The struggle for power in the Far East between Japan and Russia centered more on Manchuria than on Korea; however, Korea suffered more in the aftermath of the Russo-Japanese war of 1904–1905 in which this rivalry culminated. The Japanese, in order to be militarily successful, demanded from Korea rights of passage and other strategic advantages in the Korean peninsula. The Korean court could find no way to deny its powerful neighbor and the Japanese came into Korea under the treaty rights thus obtained. A Japanese Resident-General was placed in charge of many phases of government.

The Korean King attempted without success to have the case of Korea considered at the Portsmouth (New Hampshire) Peace Conference which ended the Russo-Japanese War. However, the United States under Theodore Roosevelt gave the Koreans only short shrift; even today some Korean politicians refer, with bitterness, to the lack of American support at that time. Again in 1907 the Korean King, though he had signed an agreement in 1905 giving over to the Japanese control of Korea's foreign relations, sent envoys to the Second International Peace Conference at The Hague. But they were not admitted. The King, as a result of this attempted show of independence, was forced by the irate Japanese to abdicate in favor of his far-from-bright son.

During these years the Japanese took over more and more internal powers; the police, the army, the customs and other branches of government were controlled by Japanese. The Koreans put up minor resistance. "Righteous Armies," including some ex-soldiers, conducted a guerrilla-type warfare. Finally, on August 22, 1910, Korea was annexed outright by Japan. The Korean royal family, except for its distant members, were sent to Japan where they became a collateral family of the Japanese royalty with the head of the family a "prince." (Many years later the crown prince, an infant at the time of the annexation, was married to a Japanese royal lady, and served as a general in the Japanese army. Eventually in 1964 he was allowed to return to Korea, a serious invalid, to await death in the land of his ancestors.)

78

Japan's Colonial Rule

The Japanese ruled Korea as a colony from 1910 to 1945. The Japanese regime in Korea was always headed by a military personage, usually an Army general, though occasionally by a Navy admiral who tended to be more liberal. There were sporadic efforts on the part of the Koreans to overthrow their hated masters. Though these were ineffectual, they did serve to keep the spark of freedom alive.

The first years of Japanese rule were marked by considerable harshness. Some Koreans resisted by joining guerrilla bands in the mountainous regions, but they were eventually suppressed or driven into Manchuria and Russia. Symptomatic of the Japanese initial unsureness and fear of Korean revolt was the Conspiracy Case which was brought to trial in 1912. The case was based on a faked charge that an American missionary, George Shannon McCune, had joined with a group of Koreans in conspiring to assassinate the Japanese Governor-General Terauchi. After severe torture under which some Koreans lost their lives or minds, 105 Koreans were sentenced to long prison terms. The miscarriage of justice was obvious and after a year an opportunity arose for the Japanese to release 99 of them quietly. (The next week the writer of this book was born and was given as his Korean name, Yun Anpaek "the peaceful hundredth one"!)

A serious effort on the part of the Koreans to declare their independence was made in the *Mansei* movement of March 1, 1919. The old Korean King, the one who had abdicated in 1907, died on January 22, 1919, and his burial was arranged for March 3. This provided an opportunity for gatherings in Seoul and for inconspicuous movement of messengers and leaders throughout Korea. News of President Wilson's fourteen-point declaration proclaiming the doctrine of self-determination of peoples for nationhood had spread among the

79

intelligentsia of Korea at the end of World War I. Exiled Koreans in China and the United States and Korean students in Japan discussed their nationalistic desires with fervor. The Chundogyo, the native Korean religious group, was contacted and it provided funds and printing facilities to help in the movement. Christian leaders abjuring force and insisting that only peaceful demonstrations should be held were also involved. These groups had effective means of communication and were important in furthering the movement, though it should be stressed that it was not a religious movement but a political one.

A Declaration of Independence, in reality an appeal for a redress of wrongs, was written by a famous author, Choe Namson, and signed by thirty-three Korean leaders, including Christian pastors, Chundogyo officials, and Buddhist monks. Twenty-nine of the thirty-three gathered in a restaurant in Seoul on March 1, 1919, and sent the declaration to the Japanese Governor-General and gave themselves up for arrest. Simultaneously, young Koreans read the declaration to throngs gathered in Pagoda Park and in other places in Seoul and throughout Korea. They led the people in shouting *"Tae han* (or *"Choson")* *tongnip mansei."*—"May Korea be free for ten thousand years." This was often shortened to *Mansei*, the same characters as the Japanese *banzai*. On March 1st and on the days that immediately followed, over a million Koreans were involved in shouting "Mansei," according to official Japanese sources. Korean historians double the figure. These people were from all ranks of society and from all regions of Korea, a very broadly based national manifestation for freedom.

Japanese authorities, caught off guard and in relative panic, set about harshly suppressing the movement. They arrested thousands of persons. It became a matter of great personal pride for Koreans to be arrested; after shouting, many paraded to police stations asking for arrest. In some cases violence broke out and Koreans were shot or tortured to death. Using the royal funeral as an excuse, stores in Seoul closed their doors and were finally opened under police pressure after three or four weeks. Some villages were burned and Korean mobs on some occasions turned on the Japanese police and stoned them to death. But by and large it was a pacifist movement. The only weapons the Koreans had were their voices and they shouted "Mansei" until they were hoarse.

Obviously the desired results were not obtained. The Peace Conference, to which Koreans in exile sent a small delegation, did not consider the Korean case for self-determination, since Japan was a member of the Conference and claimed this was a domestic matter. The Koreans in exile in Shanghai and in the United States followed the movement by organizing a provisional government and a commission to press the case for independence. These organizations were never strong and had only the most tenuous ties with potential leaders in Korea. However, throughout Korea the spark of hope of the Korean people for freedom was fanned anew and branded deep in their memories the echoes of the shouts of Mansei remained.

Though they did not, for fear of showing weakness, react immediately, the Japanese government did make changes. A more liberal Governor-General, Admiral Saito, was appointed. He eased the harshness of the Japanese rule and fostered cultural movements. Some Koreans began to feel that perhaps through education and through cooperation with the Japanese in economic spheres they might achieve a better life and make Korea and the Koreans stronger. More freedom was given to the Korean press, though it was still controlled and newspapers were suppressed from time to time. The police were put under civilian rather than military control and, for example, Japanese police who learned Korean were given salary bonuses. The Japanese effectively kept under surveillance any organized groups which had hostile attitudes toward Japan.

Some Koreans looked to communism as their salvation. As compared to the relatively stronger group among the Korean students in Japan and the Koreans in Manchuria and Russia, the Communist party members within Korea were very few in number. They tried to stir up a movement on June 10, 1926, to parallel that of March 1, 1919, the occasion being the death of the young King (who had succeeded to the throne in 1907). But this plan was known in advance by the Japanese police and never came off. The Communists attempted to join with or infiltrate other nationalistic groups in social action organizations, but were not very successful. Not only did the Japanese police watch the Communists with great care, but Korean religious and business leaders were also very suspicious of them.

In 1928 and 1929 there were some student riots which were anti-Japanese in nature, but they were quickly broken up. Some rioting was allowed, if not actually fostered, by the Japanese in the summer of 1931 to help their efforts in Manchuria. These were directed against the small handful of Chinese merchants in Korea as a protest against reported anti-Korean movements in Manchuria. Scandals of corruption in the Japanese Government-General resulted in the recall of some of the Japanese but evoked little more than mutterings by the Koreans. A renewed tightening up of military control in Korea accompanied the Japanese military moves into Manchuria in 1931. "Tough" generals were appointed to the Governor-General position in Korea and military training and defense bases were increased. The peninsula served as a staging area for the war in China that started in full scale in 1937.

Though the Free World forces in World War II would have liked to have formed a fifth column in Korea, this was not possible because of the tight Japanese control and the lack of contacts with potential leaders. The handful of exiles abroad in Washington, Chungking and Yenan, were useful to the Allied cause, but they had very limited effectiveness. Decisions about Korea and its future were guided in general by the desire to punish Japan and strip her of all of the areas, including Korea, which she had gained from her military aggressive policy of the prewar decades.

Modernization of the Economy

During this period of Japanese control Korea had, of course, undergone not just political domination but vast economic and social changes. Some of these were the products of the times, some were due to Japanese policies. It is hard to separate the two. Some students of the period feel that economic progress would have been more accelerated with a free Korea. Others consider that Japanese planning and administration plus Japanese capital should be given some credit for this transformation. No matter the weight given to the causal factors, the results are evident. The old traditional Korean economy was drastically modified and changed in the modern era.

One important factor was population. Gradually over the centuries Korea's population had been increasing. According to the available tax roll figures in 1693, there were roughly 7,000,000 people in Korea. This figure was probably much lower than the actual census since it was related to taxation; some persons estimate it at only half the actual number. For the next two centuries population leveled off with periodic fluctuations due to famine and pestilence. There were few controls over such disasters as local floods or droughts and epidemics. The Korean society was geared to a large birth rate, with honor going to the fertile wife who could produce sons to perpetuate the family.

The Japanese introduced modern public health measures,

83

controlling epidemics and improving transportation so that food could be brought into famine or flood-stricken districts. These measures led to a sharply reduced death rate. At the same time changes in the social mores that might have led to a diminishing birth rate were not forthcoming. The result was a sudden rise of population from an estimated 13,000,000 or 14,000,000 at the start of the period of Japanese control (1905) to 19,523,000, at the first official census in 1925. By 1944 the population reached 25,900,000. (This figure includes some 780,000 civilian Japanese.)

Along with this growth there were some shifts in population distribution. The pioneer lands of north Korea attracted some. However, the southern plains and river valleys were still the dominant locale of population. Many people moved to the towns and new cities. A number of these, such as Sinuiju and Taejon, had grown up along rail lines, particularly in the latter part of the Japanese period; others, like Hamhung and Chongjin, developed around industrial centers. The major cities of the past, Seoul, Pyongyong, and Taegu, also expanded rapidly. The ports—Pusan, Inchon, Wonsan, and Kunsan—developed from small fishing villages into modern cities.

Another way in which the traditional Korean way of life was transformed was that agriculture began to be commercialized. In past centuries the Korean farming and fishing village had been relatively self-sufficient. Barter of goods and labor was the normal method of transaction. Under the Japanese a modern money economy was introduced, so that wages and values of farm products were expressed in *yen* and *sen*. With the greater pressure of population more intensive farming was practiced, though it still demanded great amounts of hand labor. Commercial fertilizer and extensive irrigation projects were required and these cost money. Moreover, Korean farmers were urged to produce rice and other agricultural

84

products to be sold for export to Japan. In some years as much as half of the Korean rice harvest was sent to Japan. In turn, millet and other grains were imported from Manchuria to be sold as food to the Korean farmers. The rice market in Japan was not a steady one. If there were crop failures in Japan, rice was demanded from Korea no matter what the Korean supply. In bountiful harvest years in Japan (which often coincided with bountiful harvests in Korea) the price of Korean rice was very low and Korean farmers suffered correspondingly.

Under this system of commercial agriculture, most Korean farmers lost the ownership of their lands. For example, often the assessment for irrigation projects was so great that the farmer sold one or two of his plots to pay for it; eventually he lost all his land and became a tenant. Korean landlords collaborated with Japanese rice-purchasing companies to increase their holdings. Farm lands which were reclaimed from tidal flats or which were developed for irrigation became the property of development corporations, such as the Japanese government-owned Oriental Development Company. The workers on these lands were tenants or seasonal laborers. Because of the growing population pressure, the Korean farmers could not resist this economic exploitation. Thus, by 1938, only 18 percent of the farm families owned their own land, 24 percent owned some land and rented the rest, 52 percent were tenants, a little less than 4 percent were farm laborers, and a little more than 2 percent were tillers of land they had cleared by fire in the mountain areas. The farm land used per farm family had also decreased so that by 1938 only 17 percent of the farms were more than six acres and 38 percent were less than one and one-fifth acres in size.

Some reforestation projects were attempted by the Japanese but were not very successful. The wood-hungry Korean farmers and their sons cut branches and raked pine needles and leaves to provide household fuel. In the periods of "spring hunger" in some destitute districts, farm families even ate the bark of trees. The results of this overexploitation, plus the lack of preventive measures against insect pests and erosion, devastated the forests, especially near densely populated areas. Bare hills with gully erosion became commonplace. In the northern interior of Korea the Japanese engaged in commercial forestry. Great rafts of timber were floated down the Yalu and Tumen rivers and Sinuiji became a sawmill and exporting center, but the Koreans benefited very little from this industry.

Fishing had been a traditional part-time occupation of fisher-farmers along the coasts. When the Japanese introduced modern boats and nets, commercial fishing centered itself in a few large ports and local fishermen could no longer compete. The fishing grounds for sardines along the east coast were overfished; in 1938 a million tons of sardines were landed, in 1940 the catch was negligible.

Associated with traditional agricultural, forestry, and fishing had been handicraft industries. These were part-time or off-season occupations in which Korean farmers and fishermen made straw shoes, rope, fishing nets, and so on. Certain villages or families in a village would specialize in making clay pots or simple farm equipment, like plows or sickles. Housewives became skilled in weaving cotton and silk; their products beyond the family needs were bartered at the town fairs. Increased commercialization brought radical changes. Local handicrafts could not compete against cheap manufactured articles from Japan like rubber shoes and farm utensils. New methods had to be found to earn money, not only to pay taxes and rents, but to buy these necessary products. People were driven to selling their agricultural products and, piece by piece, their precious land. The traditional Korean economy was drastically transformed, never to recover.

86

Outside of agriculture, the Koreans had never exploited the natural resources of the peninsula on a large scale. Some iron ore production, more gold mining, largely from alluvial deposits, and small production of precious stones, such as crystal, were all that they had undertaken. To meet modern industrial demands the Japanese searched the land for valuable mineral resources. What little they found they developed, but sometimes on an uneconomic basis, particularly as Japan's war machine created demands.

Gold was of particular importance in the pre-World War II days for its value in foreign exchange. Large dredges or hydraulic systems were used in the alluvial gold deposits. Some shaft mines to exploit complex deposits were dug at scattered locations. A mine in northwestern Korea that had been worked by an American company under an original concession from the Korean King was finally sold to Japanese interests in 1941. During World War II, when Japan no longer needed foreign exchange, gold mining came to a virtual halt.

Korea produced a number of minor minerals, notably crystalline graphite and, more importantly, amorphous graphite. Especially in the last years of Japanese control, Korea became one of the world's leading producers of graphite. The mines were scattered in the mountain areas. Tungsten had a similar distribution and trend of production since it was highly valued as an alloy during the war. Copper, lead, zinc —sometimes mined in association with complex gold ores— and manganese were of some importance.

Anthracite coal in low-grade deposits occurs in a number of places in Korea. Over a million tons were produced annually in the five years before World War II. Much of this which came from the area around Pyongyang in northwestern Korea and Samchok in southeastern Korea was exported to Japan. Bituminous coal had to be imported from Manchuria and North China for use in railroad engines, thermal power

87

plants and industrial factories. Brown coal (or lignite) was mined in northeastern Korea, giving large tonnages of poor value.

Small deposits of iron ore had been mined by Koreans for centuries, but large-scale mining of iron ore began during the later part of the Japanese regime. New methods of enrichment enabled the exploitation of the low-grade magnetic ore of the Musan area in the Tumen valley in extreme northeastern Korea. By 1944, over a million tons of iron ore emerged annually from this mining area and another two million tons from other scattered areas in northern Korea. South Korea produced only 100,000 tons in 1944. From these iron ore resources, coking coal imported from Manchuria, and the hydroelectric power of northeastern Korea, grew an important iron and steel industry (though modest by world standards) near Pyongyang in the northwest and in Songjin and Chongjin in the northeast of Korea.

All this exploitation of mineral resources, and the smelting, refining, and fabricating industries associated with them, was in a sense exotic to the economy of the Korean people. The capital and the engineering skills were imported from Japan and the products exported to Japan. As previously mentioned, some industries had been operated in a relatively uneconomic manner as a part of Japan's war economy.

Equally foreign to the traditional Korean way of life was the electric power industry. Koreans had used water as a source of power but only in very primitive ways, such as one method of grinding grain in which water fell and tipped a hollowed-out log at one end of a fulcrum, then spilled out again so that the other end of the log pounded into a hollowed stump. The first electric power plants to provide for home and office lighting and for streetcars in the major cities were based upon thermal power derived from coal. In the later period of their control, the Japanese expanded the thermal electric plants in the major cities and built a large plant at the Yongwol coal field in southeastern Korea.

Japan also focused its attention on the hydroelectric power resources, particularly in northern Korea. The Yalu River and its tributaries were a major area of development. A master plan called for seven large-scale projects, though only four were completed before World War II curtailed this plan. The largest dam in the Far East was built across the lower Yalu at Supung. This 640,000 kilowatt capacity plant provided power equally to Manchuria and Korea. Two of the tributary rivers of the Yalu in northeastern Korea were dammed. From lakes thus formed the water was diverted by giant tubes through the mountains and down the sharp escarpment to the coastal lowlands. Three hydroelectric power systems of 326,500, 309,800, and 200,375 kilowatt installed capacity were built to provide power for new chemical and steel industries along the northeast coast. Small hydroelectric plants grew up on the upper Han River in central Korea and on other rivers in southern Korea. Most of the development, however, took place in North Korea where heavy and chemical industries were being encouraged by the Japanese government.

Industry in Korea was almost wholly spurred by Japanese initiative and demands. Though some Korean capital was involved, it was chiefly Japanese capital which built up consumer goods industries in central and south Korea. They were based on cheap Korean labor or on nearness to the raw materials and markets. For example, plants for rice milling and breweries, and the manufacturing of cotton textiles, rubber shoes, cigarettes and patent medicines were developed in the cities or ports. Some training was offered to Koreans, but the managerial and technical skills were largely imported from Japan.

Based upon mineral and hydroelectric resources, some heavy industry was begun, particularly in northern Korea. The larg-

est chemical industrial complex in the Far East arose at Hungnam on the east coast. Cement plants near Pyongyang, oil
refineries in Wonsan, and other scattered industrial centers
along the northeast coast and at Sinuiji at the mouth of the
Yalu were indications of the emphasis upon heavy industry
in North Korea. All of these industries were a part of Japan's
war economy and were dependent on Japanese development,
management and markets. They had little connection with
or concern for the traditional basic economy of Korea.

In order for this industrial and commercial complex to
function, the Japanese built numerous ports. Some on the
west coast had tidal basins because of the thirty-foot tides.
A railroad and highway network designed, in part, for military use was developed in Korea. The traditional way of carrying of burdens in Korea is with the *chige,* or back frame in
the rough form of an A with broad straw ropes for shoulder
bands. (The American GI term "A-frame" has actually become an alternate in the Korean speech to the Korean word
chige!) A Korean with a wooden chige well-balanced on his
back can carry amazingly heavy loads. Korean women carried
bundles or water jars on their heads with a small woven mat
underneath to protect their heads and to aid in the balancing.
It is still quite common to see a Korean woman threading her
way through a crowded town street, hands swinging easily at
her sides, as she gracefully carries a jar or basket on her head.
For very heavy loads, such as straw sacks of grain, two- or
four-wheeled ox-drawn carts were used traditionally in Korea;
gradually trucks and motorcycle trucks began to replace these.
In the early days cart roads ran from villages to the towns,
but most of the transport network was made up of foot paths
along the ridges that separate the rice paddies and the dry
fields. With the import of the railroad, the car, the truck, the
motorcycle and the bicycle, the transportation system under
the impetus of the Japanese was drastically changed.

Korea was opened in the days when railroads were becoming the basic means of transport throughout the world; the Korean rail network therefore preceded the highway network. A major line, standard gauge, was built from Pusan in the southeast to Sinuiji in the northwest. This line passed through the major cities of Taegu, Seoul and Pyongyang. From Seoul a line was extended to Wonsan on the east coast and on up the northeast coast to Chongjin, whence over the hills into the Tumen valley and following this back to the coast. From Taejon, a new city south of Seoul, a line was extended southwest to the port of Mokpo. In this way the main railroad system resembled an offset X. Numerous branch lines were built to connect this system to ports or to tap the interior. A line was projected, but never completed, down the southeast coast. A new line was built across the waist of Korea connecting Wonsan with Pyongyang in the late 1930's. A supplementary rail line was built in the south going north from Pusan and into Seoul from the east. The resulting total railroad network served well to knit together the major areas of population and production.

The highway pattern paralleled the railroads and in addition many feeder roads were built. In the later part of the Japanese-control period a major road building program was engineered for the use of buses and trucks. Roads were less costly than railroads, particularly in the mountainous areas of Korea. Naturally, the expanding cities needed extensive street construction and in some larger cities much effort was expended to broaden the streets for streetcars and, later, buses. It was only in the cities that streets were paved, the major highways usually being only gravel surfaced.

Social Changes

The political and economic transformation of Korea at the hands of the Japanese was matched by a social transforma-

91

tion. Much of this was accomplished through the introduction of a modern educational system. Schools were built in the major cities and gradually education in the rural areas was expanded. There were in reality two educational systems, one for Japanese with instruction in that language and attended by a very few Koreans, and the other for Koreans in the Korean language with a major part of the curriculum taught in the Japanese language. Eventually in the late 1930's the Korean schools were required to give almost all their instruction in Japanese. There was great disparity in the amount of financial assistance given by the government, the Japanese schools being heavily favored on a per-student basis. Curriculum, textbooks, teacher certification, and space requirements were prescribed by the government and served to keep the Korean schools in line with Japanese educational policy. Heavy emphasis was given, for example, to Japanese history and literature with strong nationalistic bias. The aim was to make Korean students into Japanese citizens.

Some Korean schools were supported by Korean groups and, more particularly, by Christian church groups. These schools had to conform strictly to the Japanese government standards and curriculum, though they were allowed to give, in addition, some religious instruction. Starting in 1935 great pressure was put on the Christian schools to send their faculties and students to the Japanese Shinto shrines as a part of a program for building up pro-Japanese nationalistic fervor. Some missionaries refused to condone this practice, feeling that it was a negation of their Christian principles. They closed their schools and colleges rather than take part in such ceremonies.

The demand for education was very strong, for Koreans felt that it was only through education that their children could attain economic and social status and a measure of freedom. To provide this education they went to great efforts and made great sacrifices. Unfortunately, facilities were inadequate and financial resources meager. Part-time programs such as boys' clubs in the cities, village reading schools during the winter months and literacy programs in connection with Christian churches were often the only educational opportunities open to many people. They scarcely satisfied the real hunger which the Korean people had for learning.

Though the Christian movement had penetrated Korea when the country was opened to the outside world, it was during the period of Japanese rule that it made great strides. In the face of an uncertain and fast-changing world Koreans were searching for spiritual sustenance. Christianity offered much. Moreover, for some Koreans the Christian churches and associated educational and social welfare programs provided a sphere of positive action that counterbalanced their frustration and restiveness under Japanese control. The Protestant missionary programs, and in a different manner the Catholic programs, were developed on sound lines with great emphasis upon indigenous leadership and financial support.

Both the Catholic and Protestant churches were organized geographically so as to avoid competition between sects or the national origins of the missionaries. The Catholic Missions, for example, had German Benedictine missionaries in the northeast, American Maryknoll missioners in the northwest, French Catholic fathers in the central part of Korea, Irish Columban fathers in the south, and so on. The American Northern Presbyterians were in north and central Korea, American Southern Presbyterians were in the southwest, Canadian Presbyterians in the northeast and Australian Presbyterians in the southeast. The Presbyterians and Methodists very early drew a map of Korea separating the areas in which they would organize churches. Thus, if a Korean Protestant convert moved, he changed his church denomination. This system meant that for many years there was not, with isolated exceptions, the situations of competing Protestant religious organizations which appeared to hold back missionary work in some other parts of Asia.

Christianity was relatively important in Korea. The city of Pyongyang, for example, had more Christians than any other city of any size in Asia. In terms of the total population, however, in the years just before World War II less than 5 percent of the Korean population was Christian. Naturally, the Japanese did not aid the Christian missionary work in Korea, they barely tolerated it. They maintained close surveillance over the Christian leaders, particularly after the Mansei movement of 1919, in which Christian pastors played a prominent role. In some instances, for example on the Shinto Shrine issue in 1936, the Japanese virtually forced certain missionaries to resign. As World War II progressed, the Japanese, seeking to control the thinking of all citizens, forced the merger of the Christian churches into one overall organization under docile leadership.

There was not much fervent religious feeling among the mass of the Korean people. In times of sickness and trouble visits might be made to a Buddhist temple, where the spirits of the dead were propitiated through routine and sometimes elaborate ceremonies. The Japanese gave some support to Buddhist temples, particularly to the same sects which were strong in Japan. The deep and pervasive nature worship which characterized the Korean people continued, particularly in the rural areas. Women continued to consult with the local mudang, or sorceress, to cleanse the home of evil spirits. Men in the scholar class continued to discuss and train their sons to follow Confucian ethics, but with less success under the Japanese. Chondogyo—the indigenous religious movement of the 1890's—still had some followers, but the Japanese were suspicious of this native religion with its nationalistic overtones. Generally speaking, the bulk of the Korean people were fast losing the religious and ethical bases to their lives. The Japanese Shinto Shrines and the enforced patriotic devotion to a distant and Japanese Emperor-God drew only a superficial and forced response from the Koreans.

Under Japanese control Korea developed more and more into a police state. The Koreans were already accustomed to the oppressive measures of the "runners" of the magistrates, who often used harsh methods such as beatings to punish wrongdoers. There was strong feeling in the villages against outside government officials who appeared only as rapacious tax collectors; government was only a necessary evil and not a help to the common people. The Japanese government in Korea had not only to oppose apathy and distrust of all officialdom on the part of the Koreans but to face outright, though rarely vocal, hostility because they represented an alien cultural force imposed upon the Koreans. A resentful people, the Koreans under the Japanese had little respect for law and order, for it represented the hated Japanese. After the Mansei movement of 1919, it became a matter of pride, not of social disgrace, to have spent time in a Japanese prison —no matter what the crime. Inevitably many Koreans, trusting no one, became amoral. They were kept in a state of law and order only through fear of the police, not through any feeling of personal responsibility for community welfare. In the judgment of some, the moral disintegration that took place among the Korean people during these days of Japanese rule has proved to be one of the great tragedies of Korea.

The end of World War II and the collapse of the Japanese control left a Korea ill-equipped to face a modern world. The Japanese had suppressed the political aspirations of the Koreans and allowed for no training in political leadership. The modern economy of Korea had been geared increasingly to the Japanese war economy and much of it was unsuitable to a peacetime atmosphere. Population growth was putting tremendous pressure on the basic economic structure. Most of the land, the natural resources, the manufacturing industry, and the commercial establishments had been in the hands of the Japanese. Few Koreans possessed high-grade technical and business skills. Education had been limited in amount and in level. The moral fiber of the bulk of the Korean people had weakened through the decades of living in a police-dominated state. Koreans hated the Japanese and passionately wanted their freedom but had little concept of the responsibilities and duties that must be assumed by the citizen under modern democratic self-government. It was, thus, a confused and a poorly prepared citizenry with serious economic and social problems who faced freedom in a complex world in August of 1945.

VII.   The Korean War

The Korean War was a result of a chain of events and pressures which occurred not just in the Korean peninsula but in the councils of nations, some of them far distant from the Korean peninsula. It created devastation throughout Korea and is a bitter memory to all Koreans. The Korean War marked the first time that the United Nations undertook military action. Though most of the UN troops were Republic of Korea and United States soldiers, they were joined by fifteen United Nations members who sent troops and military supplies. The United Nations by its actions in the Korean War used military force to preserve world peace and to halt aggression. In so doing it changed the UN organization from an ineffective debating society to a dynamic agency for world peace.

More than an international incident, the Korean War was a shattering experience which changed the lives of all of the Korean people. It brought tragedy to every Korean north and south of the 38th parallel. Millions lost their lives and cherished property. Millions were uprooted and had to make new homes amidst new surroundings. New patterns of family life, of society, of economy, and of political life evolved as a result of the war.

The Korean War is still an unfinished war, a war without victory. Only a military armistice, with a Truce Line bordered on each side by a two-kilometer no-man's-land, has stopped the fighting. Half a million soldiers, with many more forces and weapons ready to back them up, are poised on each side of the demilitarized zone that cuts across the peninsula. These forces are constantly probing each other and keeping their defenses alert. Meetings lasting from a few minutes to many hours are held by the Armistice Commission and provide a sounding board for propaganda and for the refutation of allegations concerning violations of the Armistice.

The 38th Parallel

The unfortunate division of Korea at the end of World War II in part caused the Korean War. In August 1945 Japan had been defeated and there was a need for a line to separate areas for the acceptance of the surrender of the Japanese forces. The chosen line, the 38th parallel, was not designed nor intended to be a political dividing line. The historical precedent (when the Japanese proposed to the Russians in 1903 that this parallel be used to separate spheres of influence) was an obscure event and quite likely played no part in the decision, at least insofar as the Americans were concerned. In the west the line had the advantage to the United States of leaving Seoul in the southern sector, but it went right through the northern edge of the city of Kaesong and cut in half some other towns and villages. In the west it separated the Ongjin Peninsula from the mainland. In the east the line went across the grain of the land, up and down mountains and valleys. As a parallel of latitude, it had no

98

relation to the terrain and was very difficult to defend from a military standpoint. The tragedy of the 38th parallel is that for its original purpose—a military expedient clearly marked on maps—the line thus drawn was acceptable, but as a political boundary between opposing political forces, it was a totally unnatural choice.

South Korea

The Americans, upon entering Korea south of the 38th parallel at the end of World War II, made an initial error. To make their task easier, they decreed that the Japanese authorities should be kept in office until they could be replaced. This aroused a storm of protest from the Koreans. Korean leaders, with the blessing of the Japanese, who feared rioting and chaos, had formed committees for law and order. These were not recognized by the Americans but they did rescind their decisions to use the Japanese. An American military government was hastily set up although the Americans had no desire for a military occupation of Korea, far distant from their shores. It was hoped, perhaps naively, that in due course, after the military phases of Japan's defeat were completed, negotiations would take place to unify a free and independent Korea.

Thus, at a Moscow meeting of foreign ministers in December, 1945, a joint US-USSR Commission was organized to work toward the unification of Korea. This Commission, meeting in Seoul in the spring of 1946, was blocked by the adamant Soviet position not to recognize as "democratic" many Korean groups who had voiced opposition to the setting up of the Commission, though some of the groups even in the Soviet-controlled areas of Korea had done so before they "heard the word." The Commission, therefore, recessed but after lengthy negotiations was reconvened in the spring of 1947. Again it met with failure as the Russians held to their intransigent attitude and as the United States, beginning to recognize that the real interest of the Communists was in domination, took a less conciliatory attitude. Still desirous of a unified and independent Korea, the United States put the Korea problem to the United Nations in the fall of 1947.

The United Nations appointed a temporary commission in Korea to bring about the unification of the country and to oversee elections for a constituent assembly to form an independent Korean government. Since the United Nations Commission was not allowed to enter North Korea, it was forced to restrict its efforts to the area south of the 38th parallel. Here a constitution was drafted by a selected group of Korean leaders and under it elections were held in the summer of 1948. The Republic of Korea (ROK) thus formed was given recognition by the United States and other nations.

The United States had been carrying on a military occupation of the zone south of the 38th parallel. Some features of this occupation were excellent, for example, the development of literacy campaigns and basic educational systems. Other features were not so effective, for example, the delay in instituting needed land reform programs. In the initial phases there was need for a limited program of civilian relief. This was accomplished with typical American generosity. Fortunately, very little war damage had harmed the peninsula. However, many Korean repatriates from Japan and Japanese-occupied areas had to be absorbed into the Korean economy and society. In addition, some 2,000,000 persons, over one-fifth of the population of North Korea, had moved south escaping from the Communist rule. Some of these migrants were Christians or others whose ideology could not coexist with that of the Communist regime which was taking over. Others were small landholders who were dispossessed of their lands in a harshly-imposed land reform movement. Some of these refugees were older persons who wished to be with their families, even though distantly related, in the south. It was difficult to absorb such large numbers of people into the life of South Korea.

A number of Koreans who had been keeping alive the flame of independence in foreign lands had also returned. Among these was a group, the Provisional Government of Korea, who had been refugees in China. Their representative in Washington, Syngman Rhee, also returned. A very interesting and intense person, Dr. Rhee had been active for many years in seeking to gain American support for Korean independence. On his return he managed to gain considerable political power, aided by certain sectors of the American occupation forces.

The various political leaders were not recognized as official representatives of the Korean people by the United States. However, they were given freedom to engage in political activity. Considerable turmoil accompanied the organizing of political parties and forces. The shifting coalitions of groups were bewildering, particularly for the American military authorities. These men were combat forces with little training for a military occupation of Korea. It was a time of travail for the Korean people who had been for decades under the harsh and rigid Japanese control. They welcomed their new freedom, but often were interested only in freedom and not in responsibility. Democratic processes were slow in being adopted.

Despite numerous difficulties, the Republic of Korea, with economic and technical support from the United States, began eventually to put together an effective government. Syngman Rhee was elected the first president and Koreans were elected or appointed to the traditional three branches of government: the legislative, judicial, and executive. (Of great assistance was a cycle of favorable weather which improved the basic agricultural economy.) There was, however, a very serious short-

101

age of leadership in all fields. A constabulary which had grown out of the police became the nucleus of a modern army, though it was not well trained. Its equipment, furnished by the United States, was limited to defensive weapons, for it was an uncomfortable fact that Syngman Rhee was often calling for "a march north" to unify his country by force.

North Korea

North of the 38th parallel, the Russians, having entered Korea as a part of their very short military action against the Japanese, recognized the existing Korean committees. However, they infiltrated them with their own cadre of Russian-trained Korean Communists. These Communists, led by Kim Ilsung, a former Soviet military officer, gradually took over. This enabled the Russians to remain in the background and still exercise complete control. In 1948, at the same time that the ROK was established in the south, the Soviet Union organized out of the Korean committees, the Democratic People's Republic of Korea. To this regime Communist China and other communist states, also, extended recognition and support.

The North Korea regime tried in numerous ways to block the development of the Republic of Korea. Electric power which had been furnished to the south in large amounts was cut off in 1948. There was a constant, though not too effective, barrage of propaganda demands for "elections" and for the withdrawal of the United States "imperialist" armed forces. North Korea sought to build up its own economy. The flight of over 2,000,000 persons to the south gave some relief to the population pressure. Land reforms were instituted and initially had a favorable effect on agricultural production. Military forces were strengthened. The Communists sent many young men to the Soviet Union for military and technical training. Others went to Communist-held areas of Manchuria

102

where they joined Communist armies fighting against the Nationalist Chinese forces. They gained their military training, especially in guerrilla tactics, in the field. Finally, the North Koreans with the assistance of their Soviet Russian advisors and using Soviet equipment, including heavy tanks, turned to military aggression to unify Korea.

The Communist Aggression

The first Communist moves on June 25, 1950 were remarkably successful. The ROK troops along the 38th parallel were quickly overrun and bypassed; Seoul was given up after sporadic fighting. The ROK troops were forced to blow up the bridge across the Han River, even while a stream of civilians was crossing it. Masses of Koreans, civilian and military, fleeing south added to the general chaos and confusion. Those ROK troops which had remained under a semblance of discipline were difficult to organize and were not able to provide an effective counter-defense against the North Korean advance. Korean political leaders and government officials moved south, though some of them also were captured and taken north; efforts to trace them have met with little success.

The political reaction in Washington and at the United Nations was to name Douglas MacArthur, the U. S. Commanding General in Japan, as the commander of United Nations forces to assist the ROK in meeting the Communist aggression. The ROK troops were put under UN operational control. American officers and some troops were flown in; the military action began to resemble a retreat more than a rout. Some delaying tactics were successful, but it was not possible for the UN to put up an effective defense until they were able to organize their forces along the Naktong River in southeastern Korea. Through the beachhead at the port of Pusan, supplies and troops began to flow from the United States and from American bases in Japan and in Okinawa.

Troops of other nations joined the UN forces. Some of them, the Turks and British for example, furthered their excellent reputations as fighting forces during the Korean War. During the hot and rainy summer, battles were waged along the Naktong in which the Communists attempting to cross the river were thrown back in bitter fighting. The North Koreans came to depend more and more upon hastily recruited troops as their Manchurian field-trained soldiers were lost at a high rate. Their supply lines were long and the speedy victory they had expected over the ROK troops did not materialize as they confronted United States-led troops and material.

The United Nations Offensive

The war shifted dramatically on September 15, 1950, when the United States Tenth Army Corps, supported by U. S. Marine and Navy forces and ships, made a landing at Inchon on the east coast eighteen miles from Seoul. This brilliant military move, planned, organized, and carried out in spite of great odds, caught the Communist enemy by surprise. Bitter fighting took place in the streets of Seoul. Parts of the city were burning when General MacArthur and President Syngman Rhee made a triumphant entry on September 29, three months after the city had been lost to the Communist aggressors.

Coinciding with the Inchon landings and the cutting of the supply lines by the taking of Seoul, the UN forces broke out of the Pusan perimeter. ROK troops which had been reorganized moved directly north, UN forces moved westward and northward. This time it was the Communist troops who were demoralized and ill-equipped. Many of their units were at only half or quarter strength. Their soldiers disappeared into the hills or were captured by UN forces. The North Korean aggressors had been met and defeated in the plains and hills of South Korea. Though some troops were able to retreat northward, the bulk of the North Korean forces had lost their lives or had been captured in the collective action of the UN troops.

A new time of decision then arrived. Should the UN forces advance northward beyond the 38th parallel? Though it is not too clear which event took place first, ROK troops did follow fleeing Communist soldiers across the 38th parallel in early October and on October 7 the United Nations General Assembly resolved that "all appropriate steps be taken to ensure conditions of stability throughout Korea." Interpreting the resolution as allowing them to do so, UN forces advanced northward. The Eighth Army captured Pyongyang, the North Korean capital, and sent large forces northward along the railroad toward Sinuiju on the Yalu. Other spearheads went inland up into the northern interior. The Tenth Corps crossed from Seoul to Wonsan and advanced northward along the east coast with spearheads into the interior. One of these groups reached the Yalu River at Hyesanjin.

The New War

The Chinese Communists looked on these UN advances as a serious threat to their own security. On October 1, Mao Tse-tung had said, "The Chinese people will not tolerate foreign aggression and will not stand aside if the imperialists wantonly invade the territory of their neighbor." The Chinese were particularly concerned as the UN and ROK troops neared the Yalu. Therefore, they went into action. Massive forces of so-called "volunteers" slipped across the Yalu and formed units in the mountain valleys of North Korea. In mid-November roughly 180,000 Chinese troops were facing the Eighth Army and 120,000 more troops were poised against the Tenth Corps. The first Chinese were taken prisoner in late October, but the UN commanders did not believe that massive Chinese intervention was taking place. They were lured on and were entrapped by the Chinese who began their offensive and started, in the words of General MacArthur, "an entirely new war."

The Chinese Communists had undergone long training in a type of ground warfare well suited to the Korean terrain. They moved like ghosts through the scrubby forests emerging with bugle calls and shouts in the early morning. The Chinese Communists used these bugle calls for their signal system since they had very little radio-communication equipment. Their logistics were simple compared to that of the UN forces who were tied by their heavy equipment and motor transport to roads, where they could be ambushed by forward-ranging, lightly equipped Chinese patrols. The Marines' bitter battles on the road back from the Chongjin Reservoir, the Eighth Army's crossing the Chungchon River, the Turkish Brigade's stoic defenses in the "Gauntlet," these actions and many others were heroic but of little avail against the oncoming flood of Chinese. Complete American air superiority had been maintained throughout the offensive phases of the Korean War, but it had little effectiveness in this type of "riflemen's war." The bitterly cold winter weather of the northern winter was equally an enemy to UN troops. Finally, on January 4, 1951, the city of Seoul was taken by the Chinese Communists.

The UN and ROK troops regrouped, and were joined by reserve forces brought into South Korea along a line roughly seventy-five miles south of the 38th parallel. Here the less rugged terrain was better suited to mechanized warfare and in February the UN resumed the offensive. The Chinese Communists now had long supply lines and their logistic problems became severe. The war was now a series of probes, of offenses and counter-offenses. General MacArthur had not been in accord with the major policy decisions made in Washington, for example, the denial of air strikes beyond the Yalu. This disagreement broke into the open and President Truman recalled him on April 11, 1951. He was replaced by General Matthew Ridgeway. General James Van Fleet took command of the Eighth Army in Korea. Seoul was retaken on March 18, 1951, but bitter fighting continued as the Chinese Communists dug in. The UN forces were not able to mount a fast-moving offensive in the cold mountains of central Korea.

Truce Negotiations

A year after the start of the war, the Soviet delegate to the UN, Jacob Malik, proposed a truce—perhaps in the knowledge that a strong offensive was being organized by the UN forces. This proposal was accepted by the UN command and on July 10, 1951, truce talks commenced at Kaesong and continued later at a point between the lines, the village of Panmunjom. These talks were laboriously slow. Meanwhile, severe fighting continued along the mountainous front. Names like Bloody Ridge and Heartbreak Ridge gave an indication of the bitterness of the hand-to-hand fighting that took place. A million men faced each other on the wavering battle line that stretched across the Korean peninsula just south of the 38th parallel in the west and well north of it on the east coast.

One of the points of disagreement in the tents at Panmunjom was the methods to be used for exchange of prisoners of war. Many North Koreans and Chinese Communists prisoners did not want to be repatriated. Finally, the Chinese Communists accepted an Indian proposal that the prisoners be screened by India as a neutral nation. On June 8, 1953, at Panmunjom a general agreement on repatriation was signed. Shortly thereafter the delicately balanced negotiations were almost wrecked when Syngman Rhee allowed 25,000 North Koreans to "escape" from prison camps without screening. Eventually, 75,000 Communist troops were exchanged for 12,750 UN soldiers. Another 75,000 North Korean troops chose to stay in South Korea, and 14,000 Chinese Communists chose to go to Formosa rather than to return to China. There were 21 Americans and one Briton who elected to stay in Communist China, and 327 South Koreans who stayed in North Korea.

The truce, which was finally signed on July 27, 1953, set up a military demarcation line across Korea along the line where combat had been taking place during the long months of the negotiations. A two-kilometer stretch on either side of the line became a no-man's-land. The Truce Line went at an angle to the 38th parallel but differed from it decidedly in that the local terrain provided much better defensive positions. This line, however, meant that Korea was still a divided land. Only a truce had been signed, and this was not signed by the Republic of Korea, but only by the UN commander and the Chinese Communists and their North Korean counterparts. The problem of a divided land remained, though the dividing line could be more easily defended by both sides.

The War's Effects

The Korean War was "a peculiar war" in many ways. Combat was confined to conventional rather than nuclear weapons. Many decisions were based on political considerations rather than military expedience. Strategic air power was not used against supply bases in the Communist "havens" in Manchuria. Close air support of tactical ground units gradually evolved as an effective weapon. The factor of morale, particularly among prisoners of war who were subjected to "brainwashing," was a crucial element.

The Korean War had one common character with other modern wars: devastation for the civilian population. The Korean people endured tremendous suffering and loss of human life as they were swept back and forth in the wake of the fighting. Families were separated; orphans wandered the countryside. Cities in both North and South Korea were re-

108

duced to rubble; industrial plants, railroad facilities, roads, and bridges were destroyed throughout Korea. All Koreans are bitter about the war. And many Koreans in South Korea are particularly bitter toward the Communists who started the aggression.

The Korean War is not over, though wishful thinkers like to believe so. The truce agreement called for "a political conference of a higher level of both sides" within three months after its signing "to settle through negotiations the question of the withdrawal of all foreign forces from Korea (and) the peaceful settlement of the Korean question." The Communists insisted that the Soviet Union be included as a "neutral" participant in such a conference and this condition was unacceptable to the United States. The sixteen nations who had fought in Korea under the UN flag pledged in August, 1953, to renew the war and to carry it beyond the borders of Korea if Communist aggression again occurs. From April 26 to June 15, 1954, a conference was held in Geneva of the sixteen nations and the ROK with the Soviet Union, Communist China, and North Korea. This conference made no progress whatsoever. In fact the positions were hardened. At its conclusion the same situation existed that had prevailed since 1945—a divided Korea.

Years later, Korea is still a divided land, with the Truce Line now well fortified. The ROK forces which now man the line have been well trained and equipped. Similarly trained North Korean soldiers have taken the place of the Chinese Communist forces, which have withdrawn to their havens in Manchuria. The Truce Line marking the division of Korea today continues to be an explosive and potentially dangerous front of the global cold war.

VIII. Regions of North Korea

The Democratic People's Republic of Korea (DPRK) claims jurisdiction over all Korea, though obviously it has control only over the area north of the Truce Line. Created by the Soviet Union, it has evolved into a thorough Communist state with a single leader in the Stalinist tradition, Marshal Kim Ilsung. Intervention of the Chinese Communist forces in the Korean War preserved the existence of the DPRK. Subsequently, with the split between the Chinese Communists and the Soviet Russians, the North Korean regime has seemingly cast its lot with its near and powerful neighbor, the Chinese. Never truly independent, it is becoming more and more a "younger brother" satellite of Communist China—in many respects much the same relationship as Korea had with Imperial China for hundreds of years. A highly centralized regime with a large army and with an expressed dedication to the goal of driving American "imperialists" from the Korean peninsula, it continues to pose a serious threat to the peace of the Far East and of the world.

110

Through the years since 1945, the Koreans in the north have been forced to lead a decidedly different life from that of their fellow countrymen to the south. The attacks on traditional society, the indoctrination of the young people through education, and the harassment and purging of possible dissident groups have molded North Korea into a rigid social and political entity. Possibilities of the absorption of this Communist-dominated people into a free, independent, democratic and unified Korea appear remote. The latent divisiveness between North and South Korea, occasioned by geographic and historical factors, has been sharpened. Yet under conditions of peaceful communication and action the differences between North and South Korea could give complementary strength to a unified Korea. Unfortunately, there is little that warrants any hope of such unity in the immediate future.

Geography

North Korea is a mountainous land with cold winters and limited resources. Closely tied to the continent of Asia it is continental rather than maritime in character. The Yalu and Tumen rivers form the northern border of Korea, but they cut through a mass of forbidding mountains which form the real barrier between the Korean peninsula and the Manchurian plain. The provinces and counties of North Korea have distinctive geographic characteristics but can be divided for purposes of discussion into three major regions.

The Northern Interior

The Northern Interior of North Korea is a large area of some 16,000 square miles. Its landscape is dominated by mountains and narrow, entrenched river valleys. Population is sparse and there are only a few towns. Much of the rural population is dispersed in isolated farmsteads near scattered

111

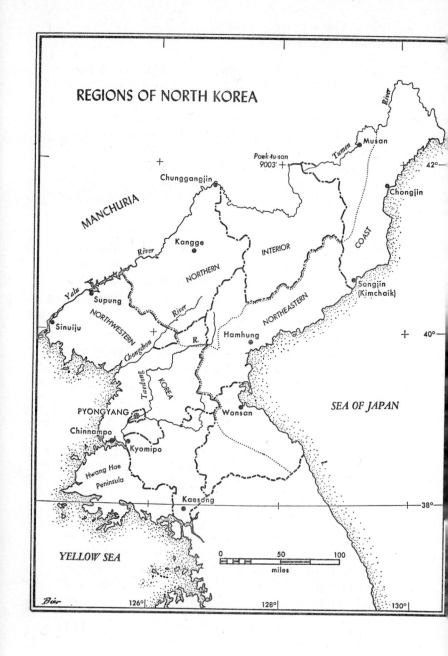

REGIONS OF NORTH KOREA

MANCHURIA

Chunggangjin

Paek-tu-san
9003'

Tumen River

Musan

Chongjin

Kangge

INTERIOR

COAST

NORTHERN

River

River

Yalu

Supung

NORTHWESTERN

NORTHEASTERN

Songjin
(Kimchaik)

Sinuiju

Chongchon

R.

Hamhung

PYONGYANG

Taedong

KOREA

Wonsan

SEA OF JAPAN

Chinnampo

Kyomipo

Hwang Hae

Peninsula

Kaesong

YELLOW SEA

0   50   100
miles

Bär

126°

128°

130°

42°

40°

38°

fields rather than in villages, as in most of Korea. The farm houses generally have wooden shingle roofs rather than thatch. Because of the bitterly cold winters the houses are built close to the ground and the fires kept going for most of the year. In recent decades some highways have been built to open up areas for mineral exploitation or for development of hydro-electric power sites, but isolation is still a major characteristic of this region. Its people have a hardy pioneering tradition which sets them apart.

In this region average temperatures are below freezing (32° Fahrenheit) for five months in the winter. Winters are dry, and though the sun does furnish some heat at midday, the winds blow bitingly cold. The January temperature along the Yalu in the middle of the region at Chunggangjin averages − 6° Fahrenheit. The summer season is short with temperatures rising only to the sixties and seventies in the valleys. It is in the months of July and August that most of the rain comes. At Chunggangjin fourteen inches is recorded on the average out of a total yearly average rainfall of thirty-two inches. Naturally, there is a great deal of variation in the climate, depending upon the elevation. Snow caps lofty Paek-tu-san (or Ever-White Mountain) for most of the year. (During the summer and early fall, pumice and other volcanic rocks at its crest look deceivingly like snow from a distance.) In the larch and pine forests that cover the mountains the snow lies deep during the winter and the rivers are tightly frozen. The rigorous weather lives vividly in the memories of those United States Marines who survived the fighting in this region in the winter of 1950–1951.

The Northern Interior has some important mineral resources—small and scattered deposits of gold, copper, and alloys for high grade steel. Near Musan, in the Tumen valley, deposits of low grade iron ore exploited by the Japanese now provide a significant resource for the North Korean economy. The larch, spruce, and pine cut from the forests on the mountain slopes in the upper drainage basins of the Yalu and Tumen rivers are floated down the rivers in the spring and summer flood stages and provide another major natural resource.

A great potential exists here for hydroelectric power. The Japanese built dams to form large reservoirs to provide water power for the northeastern coast. They also produced hydroelectric power on the Yalu and its major tributary. The largest project, with 640,000 kilowatt capacity, was at Supung, upstream about eighty miles from the mouth of the Yalu. Half of the power was sent into Korea as far south as Pyongyang, and the other half went to Manchuria, which at that time was under Japan's economic control. The Supung power plant was gutted by aerial bombing during the Korean War but has been rebuilt with Soviet equipment. It is again furnishing large amounts of electric power to both sides of the river. Other dams are reported to have been built at Kangge and other places on tributaries of the Yalu. The economy of North Korea is being developed with a high degree of dependence upon hydroelectric power, most of it derived from the water resources of the Northern Interior.

The region is the most sparsely inhabited in Korea. Total population is estimated to be between 1,000,000 and 2,000,000. There are almost no people in the mountains around Paek-tu-san and relatively few in the eastern section of the region, except at Musan and along the Tumen. Most inhabitants are widely dispersed over the western section comprised of the river valleys of the Yalu and its tributaries. This area was originally a part of the political provinces of North and South Pyongan; under the Communist regime it has been changed politically into a new province, Chagang. At river junctions or river crossings towns have developed, but there are no large cities within the region. Agricultural production is low with

114

great dependence upon hardy cereals and short-maturing rice for a subsistence livelihood. On the higher mountain slopes, sometimes at very steep grades, fields have been cleared by setting fires. Amidst the stumps and the ashes which have fertilized the soil, millet and other short-maturing cereals are grown for two or three years before the patch is abandoned and the farmer devotes his effort to newly cleared land. The farmer-squatters have little care for the land. A well-developed system of reforestation would in the long run be a better use for the land, but these "fire-field" practices are continuing under the Communist regime. Even these hardy farmers are being grouped into cooperatives through which they can be effectively controlled.

The Northeastern Coast

The Northeastern Coast of North Korea is also an isolated area, but it has a much denser population and a much more advanced economy than has the Northern Interior. The area, some 12,000 square miles, is made up of a series of valleys etched out by rivers which flow down the slopes of the Northern Interior. The most extensive valley is that of the Tumen River which forms part of the northern boundary of Korea. Another relatively large plain is around the city of Wonsan in the southern part of the region. The numerous river valleys along the coastal region are separated by intervening hills which meet the sea in headlands.

A distinctive feature of the Northeastern Coast is its maritime-influenced climate. Though it has the common characteristics of cold, dry winters and hot, wet summers that mark North Korea, the cold Liman current which flows from the north in the Sea of Japan is an ameliorating influence. The winters are not so severe as those in the Northern Interior. At the north end of the region the average January temperatures are 15° Fahrenheit, in the center they are 21° and in the south at Wonsan they are 25°. In the summer the temperatures are lower than what would be normal because of the maritime influence. The warmest month is August, rather than July, with average temperatures of 72°. Fogs are common along the coast and in some summers, when they are of long duration, crops may be retarded and fail. The rainfall is fairly heavy, especially where the coastal areas are backed by sharp escarpments. Such is the case at Wonsan which has an average annual rainfall of 53.5 inches. Most of the region has a little over half that amount. Rainfall is concentrated in a rainy season in the late summer months.

Another distinctive characteristic of the Northeastern Coast is the contrast between the agricultural and industrial economies. Traditional agricultural-based livelihood suffers from infertile soils in the small alluvial basins, and rice, cereals, and potatoes (which can survive in the cool foggy climate) are the chief crops. In contrast, modern industry, introduced by the Japanese, has flourished. Utilizing hydroelectric power, extensive chemical industries were developed at Hungnam. On the basis of iron ore from Musan and abundant power, iron and steel production and fabricating plants were built at other cities along the coastal region. Storing and packaging of imported petroleum products was handled at Wonsan in the early days of Japanese control, and later oil refineries to use imported crude petroleum were constructed there. Lignite coal deposits in the northern part of the region were liquified by the Japanese to produce kerosene and fuel oil, when imports of petroleum products were curtailed in the late 1930's.

The Japanese built a railroad along the coast utilizing the historic passageway to the south from Wonsan across the "Iron Plain" to connect this region with Seoul. In the late 1920's a new rail line went inland into the Tumen River valley, then followed it back down to the coast, and it also connected with the Manchurian rail system. After 1931 when the Japanese controlled Manchuria, they developed modern ports in this northern area of Korea, thus furnishing new access lines to Manchuria to supplement the traditional Manchurian port of Darien on the Yellow Sea. The rail lines were paralleled by highways. In addition, bus and truck routes were developed inland from the railroads to tap the Northern Interior. These were built with difficulty up and over the sharp escarpment which borders the region.

The population of this region has had a rapid growth, almost doubling between 1925 and 1944, as industry and commerce prospered under the Japanese. Some of the old fishing villages which dotted the coast lost population as fishing became concentrated in the larger ports which could handle the larger boats and nets introduced by the Japanese for commercial fishing. Traditionally, the area had been a single political province. It was subdivided by the Japanese into a northern and a southern province. With the imposition of the 38th parallel there was a further adjustment; the southernmost part was amalgamated with the area which extended south to the 38th parallel making a third political province. More recently the sections of these provinces which extended into the Northern Interior were separated to form a new province there.

During the Korean War industrial facilities, railroads, and roads were severely damaged by aerial and sea bombardment. Reconstruction of the industries of the area has had a high priority. Assistance for rehabilitation and further development, particularly for the chemical industry, came not only from the Soviet Union but from its East European satellites, such as Czechoslovakia and East Germany. Because of these changes it is difficult to estimate the population, but it may be presumed that between 3,000,000 and 4,000,000 people now live in this region. It has been somewhat favored because of its proximity to the Soviet Union and because it is a part of the home territory of Kim Ilsung and leaders in his clique who now control the government of North Korea.

Northwestern Korea

The hills and plains of Northwestern Korea are steeped in tradition. It was in this area that some of the early dynasties of Korea had their base. The earliest historical records concern a Chinese colony founded in 108 B.C. near the present city of Pyongyang. In the outskirts of that city is the reported grave of Kija, the legendary scholar who brought Chinese civilization to Korea in 1122 B.C. Certainly, the roots of the people of Northwestern Korea go deep into the earth and into the past.

The ferment, change, and destruction that has been the lot of these people in recent decades is, sadly, only a repetition of crises endured throughout many centuries. One reason is that Northwestern Korea is the contact zone between the Korean peninsula and neighboring Manchuria and China. Whenever an aggressive force has been on the loose in China, the effects on this region have been devastating. It has been a passageway, also, for culture and civilization from China. The people of this region take pride in their scholars and artists. At the same time, they consider themselves the hardy "tiger hunters" who protect the rest of Korea.

Northwestern Korea is the largest of the three geographic regions. It comprises some 19,000 square miles and has the most people, estimated between 6,000,000 and 8,000,000. It is the base region of the North Korean regime. Pyongyang, for centuries a national or provincial capital, is the political center of the Democratic People's Republic of Korea.

Within Northwestern Korea considerable geographic diversity is discernible. The major contrast is between the rugged mountainous areas on the inland borders and the

118

river plains and tidal flats along the coasts of the shallow Yellow Sea. The transition between this region and the Northern Interior is not too abrupt; the boundary has been drawn for convenience along the drainage divide between the tributary streams which flow north into the Yalu River and the streams that flow south and west into the Yellow Sea. Between this region and the Northeastern Coast the drainage divide makes the eastern boundary, though here also a maze of mountains and hills truly separates the two regions.

It is on the plains of Northwestern Korea that most of the people of North Korea make their livelihood and the major cities are located. The northern border is the Yalu River. As it nears the sea the Yalu valley broadens out into an extensive plain. For many centuries the area remained uninhabited on both sides of the river, serving as a "march" or no man's land to protect Korea; however, more recently it began to be settled. Under the Japanese, large bridges were built across the river. To the south of the Yalu are low hills and valleys. The Chongchon is the next large river. Along it some of the most severe battles of the Korean War were fought between the Chinese Communist "volunteers" and the UN forces. Still farther south is the Taedong River, the largest within the region. It has a number of tributary streams which have eaten back into the mountainous interior. The Taedong flows majestically past Pyongyang and is bordered in its lower course by extensive and densely populated plains. In the southern part of the region the Hwanghae peninsula juts out into the Yellow Sea. This section has a large area of low hills and plains, some of which were formed by the down faulting of blocks of the earth crust in past geologic times rather than by river erosion and deposition which is so common elsewhere.

The climate of Northwestern Korea is much influenced by the proximity of the region to the great plains of Manchuria and North China. The Yellow Sea is shallow and though it

119

has high tides, thirty feet and more, that have some local effect, it does not mitigate the continentality of the climate of the region. Winters are cold; January temperatures average 17.6° Fahrenheit at Pyongyang, two degrees colder to the north at Sinuiju along the Yalu River and average five degrees warmer to the south on the south shore of the Hwanghae peninsula. Summers are hot with average July and August temperatures in the upper seventies. Summers also are wet. Over half of the total yearly rainfall that averages thirty-seven inches at Pyongyang comes in July and August. This is truly a rainy season, a boon to the rice farmers provided that it comes on time and is not so concentrated as to cause floods.

Under these climatic conditions rice is the favored crop in the valleys and on the former tidal flats which have been reclaimed from the sea. On the slopes which cannot be terraced for paddy fields, cereals such as wheat, millet and grain sorghum are common. Tobacco and native cotton are also grown in areas where soil conditions and length of growing seasons permit. Many of the fields of Northwestern Korea have been tilled for centuries with great care. In recent decades, however, chemical fertilizers and improved irrigation have greatly increased production. New crops such as apples have also been successfully introduced.

Life has changed also for the industrial workers and urban inhabitants in Northwestern Korea. The factories and cities were targets for aerial attack during the Korean War and large-scale rehabilitation was a necessity. Much of this did not follow the traditional pattern but developed in new ways. The new multi-story apartment buildings, arrayed in straight rows, had the effect of drastically modifying family living.

The largest city in North Korea is Pyongyang. Its recorded history goes back over 2,000 years. Only remnants still exist of the old stone walls and gates that for centuries protected the inhabitants of the city. From its nest of hills along the north shore of the Taedong river the city has expanded in all directions: south and east across the river and north and west on to the plains of a tributary of the Taedong. The high hills are the site of a recreational park and educational center. Long rows of apartments and office buildings along the river furnish a striking contrast to the old wall and water front where rafts and boats are tied in the spring, summer, and fall.

Pyongyang was once a city where there were over 100 Christian churches and the largest body of Protestant missionaries in any city of Asia. Under communism many Korean Christians fled to South Korea; those that remained were subject to regimentation and brainwashing. The old city has seen many changes in its long history. The present circumstances, however, may be the most profound in their effect upon the architecture, form, and life of Pyongyang.

Near the mouth of the Taedong, thirty miles from Pyongyang, is the port city of Chinnampo. The high tides require floating docks, tidal gates, and basins. Warehouses line the streets of the city and the high smokestack of a copper ore refinery dominates the skyline. Salt water evaporation plots are north of the city and to the south across the estuary is the iron and steel center of Kyomipo which was developed by the Japanese early in their years of control.

The industries of Chinnampo, along with the cement mills east of Pyongyang and the numerous consumer goods and other industries in Pyongyang and its industrial suburbs, make this one of the leading industrial areas of North Korea. The hydroelectric power from the Supung dam, in addition to power from local thermal power plants, adds to the economic base of this region. This power is used at other industrial areas which have been built at sites along the rail lines extending north from Pyongyang to the Yalu River. At Sinuiju on the Yalu is another industrial center which is dependent not only upon the power resources of the river but also upon the forest products which float down it.

The Hwanghae peninsula, south of Pyongyang, had for centuries been a single political province. Under the Communist regime it has been divided into two parts as a recognition of the geographic differences. The northernmost of these two new provinces has more extensive structural plains and colder winters. Its major towns are inland marketing and transportation centers. The southern province has a small extent of alluvial plains and milder winters. The largest city in the new province, Kaesong, was an ancient capital of Korea. The old conservative scholars who used to be the city fathers and who met at the archery range or in poetry reading pavilions have been replaced by ardent young Communists.

The geographic diversity throughout North Korea needs to be recognized. Though this chapter has emphasized the three large regions—the Northern Interior, the Northeastern Coast and Northwestern Korea—into which North Korea may be conveniently divided, actually every mountain slope, every small valley has its own distinctive geographic character. Correspondingly, the North Koreans have differed from each other in history, in outlook, and in economic development. They have taken pride in their diversity and independence. Today, however, more and more their lives are regimented and through education, especially in the case of the young people, they are being recast into a common mold.

IX. Recent Developments in North Korea

In the diversified area of North Korea the Communist world has been able to develop another satellite regime. It is not large in population or resources but is of great significance because of its strategic location in the Far East. By aggression across the 38th parallel in June, 1950, the North Koreans were able to precipitate a war which almost developed into a global holocaust. Originally a creation of the Soviet Union, the Democratic People's Republic of Korea (DPRK) has in recent years become more and more an appendage of Communist China. Throughout its existence as a state it has had one leader in the Communist dictatorial tradition, Marshall Kim Ilsung. Well tutored and supported by his Soviet and Chinese overlords, he has manipulated his supporters and purged and murdered his political enemies so that he has remained in sole power. How long he may maintain this position remains to be seen, for rivalries between factions of varying compositions and strengths have been as much a part of the short history of the DPRK as they were of the longer history of Korea.

Political Developments

When the Russians first entered Korea after the Japanese collapse, they found in existence a group of "peoples' committees." They proceeded to work through them and infiltrate them with Communists who eventually took over. The leader of the committee in Pyongyang was Cho Mansik, a highly respected, venerable Korean Christian layman who was known as the Gandhi of Korea for his nonviolent resistance to the Japanese. Cho was made chief of the Five Provinces Administration Bureau, the Korean administrative organization for the area under Soviet occupation. He was aided by many Christians who gave leadership to the Korean community. They formed a political party—the Korean Democratic Party—but this was quickly infiltrated. The Communists kept it in existence to perpetuate the fiction that North Korea was a land of multiple political parties.

A handful of Korean Communists came out in the open at the time of liberation. Actually, more native Communists turned up in South Korea than in the North. The leader of the group in North Korea who collaborated with Cho Mansik was openly assassinated six weeks after the liberation. This action, obviously condoned by the Russians, served effective notice on the local Communists that they were not to be the chosen leaders of the future Communist regime.

It became apparent that the mantle of leadership was destined by the Soviets for the fat shoulders of Kim Ilsung. Born the first son of a small farmer near Pyongyang in 1912, Kim went to Manchuria when his family migrated there. At the age of 19 he joined a guerrilla band on the borders of Korea across the Tumen River. According to some accounts, there had been a guerrilla leader in the 1910's and 1920's called General Kim Ilsung. He had died in 1931 and his name had been taken by another guerrilla leader, who was killed by the Japanese in a skirmish in 1937. At this time or later Kim changed his name to become the third Kim Ilsung. Knowing the legendary stories of the original Kim Ilsung, many Koreans were surprised to see a roly-poly, baby-faced, 34-year-old Kim Ilsung when he was introduced to the people with great fanfare in October of 1945. Fabricated and highly laudatory biographies of Kim were quickly printed. They neglected to include the fact that in the 1930's Kim had moved from his guerrilla base to the Soviet Union, where he had undergone training and had served in the Soviet Army, reaching the rank of a temporary major. Kim Ilsung was a man whom the Russians felt that they could manipulate and control. By giving him the aura of a folk hero they could operate effectively behind the scenes. Along with Kim Ilsung came other Soviet-trained Korean Communists. Doffing their military uniforms they quickly infiltrated and took over local government offices, committees, and parties.

The take-over by the Kim Ilsung faction was not accomplished with ease. When the Russians instituted a forced grain procurement program, in line with their practice of living off the land they occupied, they were vigorously opposed by Cho Mansik. He also opposed the removal of industrial equipment, such as the generators from the Supung hydroelectric plant, which the Russians claimed as war booty. His major opposition was expressed at the plan for a four-power trusteeship over Korea, developed at the Moscow conference of the Big Four foreign ministers in December, 1945. He resigned from his chairmanship of the Five Provinces Administration Bureau in January and was put under house arrest by the Soviets. His ultimate fate has never been ascertained. By the time of Cho's resignation Kim Ilsung was the "people's choice" to take over the political leadership of North Korea.

In addition to the native Communist group and the Soviet-trained Communists, there was another important Communist faction—those who had been working with the Chinese Communists in Yenan. These leaders had hurried back to North Korea. Though few in number, they had been well trained and were intent on assuming leadership. Whereas the Russian-trained Communists had quickly organized local Communist parties among the landless farmers and the industrial workers, the Yenan Communists recruited landowning farmers, small businessmen and ex-government bureaucrats and teachers who had worked under the Japanese. In part, this was because of the nature of their leader, Kim Tubong, a middle-aged Korean intellectual who had left Korea in 1919. The Yenan faction was a powerful rival for early leadership in the North Korean Communist movement. At the inaugural meeting of the North Korea Workers' Party in July of 1946, though it had been expected that Kim Ilsung would be elected chairman, the strength of the Yenan group was so impressive that the Russian colonel who was manipulating the meeting arranged for Kim Tubong to be made chairman and Kim Ilsung vice-chairman. Over the years, however, the Yenan faction was progressively weakened by defection and by purges engineered by the Russian faction. Eventually in 1958, even Kim Tubong was purged.

The local Communists, after the assassination of their leader, were amalgamated into other factions but in South Korea in the early years after liberation Communists were still an important group. They were allowed to function relatively openly in Seoul and could move back and forth between North and South Korea. However, their freedom of action was curtailed in South Korea, particularly after 1948, and many of them moved north. The Seoul Communists, under leadership of Pak Honyong, had been arguing that there should be only one Communist party for all of Korea. Though this was in line with Communist theory, the Russians did not approve of it in practice, for it would tend to weaken the position of their chosen leader, Kim Ilsung. The Seoul group were given some party offices in the Korean Workers' Party, the official name of the North Korean Communist party, but eventually in 1953 Pak and his group were accused of being American spies conspiring against Kim Ilsung and were court-martialed and shot. Thus, there emerged one Communist party, the Korean Workers' Party.

The Democratic Party which had been headed by Cho Mansik, and was a rallying point for Christians and many other Koreans who were not Communist-inclined, was gradually emasculated. After Cho's downfall Communists took over the party leadership and though the Democratic Party was maintained for propaganda purposes, it had no real political power. One other non-Communist party is interesting, though it suffered the same fate as the Christian-dominated Democratic Party. This was the Chundogyo Youth Group, members of the native Korean religious sect of the 1890's, which had long had political and nationalistic overtones. It had some strength, particularly among the farming group and young people in the cities who were attracted neither to communism nor Christianity. Though this party also was preserved for some time to furnish another element for propaganda purposes in the "Fatherland Front" which had been formed in 1949, it was quickly taken over or made noneffective.

This account of the various factions and their eventual subordination to Kim Ilsung suggests that even in a monolithic Communist state factionalism may exist. Though the Kim Ilsung forces are now in power, in the future new factions may arise, fostered, for example, by Sino-Soviet rivalry. Kim Ilsung, once a Soviet puppet, has seemingly succeeded in transforming himself into a trusted ally of the Chinese Communists. The "cult of the personality" now decried in Soviet circles, though not so much so in Communist China, suits Kim Ilsung very well. One of the groups which has grown to power since

127

the Korean War is the North Korean Army. At the time of the defeat and retreat of the North Korean forces there was a major purge of army leaders; they were made scapegoats, thus diverting blame from Kim Ilsung, and in subsequent years there have been further purges in the army. Conceivably, however, as happened in South Korea, the leadership of the military forces may get more deeply involved in political affairs, particularly at a time of crisis.

Kim Ilsung not only keeps his position as leader of the Korean Workers' Party but is also Premier of the DPRK and Commander-in-Chief of the Armed Forces. The government has the usual Communist multiplicity of government offices and bureaus, including state-owned corporations of various kinds. Kim Ilsung's eventual fate will depend in large part on his ability to control the military forces and, through them and the police, the North Korean people. Much will depend upon his effectiveness in dealing with social and economic problems. Of great importance will be his relations with the Chinese Communists.

Economic Developments in Agriculture

The economy of North Korea under the Japanese was dual in character—part of it agricultural, the other industrial and urban. This duality has continued under the Communist regime. Agricultural livelihood, largely self-sufficient, was carried on by the mass of the people—three-quarters of the population, in 1946. But it did not offer an easy life. Many farmers had to till fields cleared by fire in the mountain lands or, as tenants paying rent of 50 to 70 percent of the crop, cultivate long-used soils of small plains. Some relatively extensive lands were opened up through reclamation of tidal flats and were improved by modern irrigation and drainage methods. Most of such lands, however, were owned by Japanese corporations. Liberation in the fall of 1945 coincided with good crop yields, and the farmers felt they had a double blessing. Their high hopes were soon shattered, however, when they were forced to sell their produce at low cost to the Russian Army.

To appease the North Korean farmer and to gain his acquiescence to the Communist regime, a major land reform was brought about. Large landholdings were broken up. No person or corporation could own more than 2.5 acres of farm land. The farmers who tilled the land—unless they were labeled as reactionaries—were given rights to the land. However, it was not true ownership, for they could neither sell, rent, nor mortgage their land. Enthusiasm for this program faded rapidly as high taxation in kind was imposed and donations of "patriotic rice" were exacted. Soon even the more diligent farmers were less well-off than they had been before.

The Korean War affected agricultural production seriously. Many thousands of farm workers, particularly the sons of farmers, were pressed into military service. Thousands of others escaped to South Korea, and many more thousands died from the actual fighting or the privations they underwent. An official North Korean yearbook gives the following data on population:

1946	9,257,000
1949	9,622,000
December 1, 1953	8,491,000
September 1, 1956	9,359,000
December 1, 1959	10,392,000
1960	10,789,000

This shows a drop of well over a million persons in the war years. Other estimates give the decline during the war years as 2,100,000. Another reason for the decrease in farm workers was that many joined the industrial and urban society. Though in 1946, 75 percent of the population were farmers, by 1953 only 66 percent, and by 1960, 44 percent were classed as farmers, according to official figures.

The destruction brought by the Korean War and the subsequent movement of people out of farming gave the Communist regime an opportunity to transform the agricultural sector of North Korea into a collectivist system. Some cooperatives, state farms, and tractor stations had been organized prior to November, 1954. But at that date such Communist devices began to be stressed. During the first year, half of the farmers were organized into cooperatives, another 30 percent were forced into them in the second year and by the end of the third year, December 1957, 95 percent of the farmers were thus organized. According to the official figures there were 16,000 cooperatives averaging 64 families each. By the end of 1957 all of the farmers were in 13,309 cooperatives; the drop in number was caused by the amalgamation of some of the early cooperatives.

Later, following the Chinese Communist example this amalgamation continued and cooperatives were made to coincide with political boundaries. This aided in the regimentation of the farmers and enabled the same political officials to control agricultural production who controlled other aspects of the life of the people. By 1962, the number of cooperatives was reduced to 3,843, each averaging 300 farm families. The individual farm family was allowed a small vegetable plot, chickens, and fruit trees in the farm yard. Otherwise the farm family was completely dependent upon the returns from their services given to the cooperative. The farmers were grouped into work teams and given their orders for the day by their team captain who in turn received orders from above. The North Korean farmer has to work long hours, yet he is often called on for "voluntary labor" for some special project in addition to his farm work. Incentives and punishments are used to reward the diligent and spur on the lazy worker.

130

Along with the organization of the cooperatives, state farms and tractor stations were increased in number and size, particularly where hitherto unproductive land was being turned to agriculture. To reach their goal of self-sufficiency in food production the North Korean regime found it necessary to put more land in production. According to official figures the total acres sown to cereal crops, including rice, increased from 5,613,000 acres in 1953 to 6,260,000 acres in 1957. The production per acre was also reported to have increased through the development of irrigation systems, the greater use of commercial fertilizers, and the mechanization of production. For example, tractors were used for plowing large plots and electricity powered the grain mills. It would appear that as the state farms grow, farmers' cooperatives will give way to these state farms with the individual farmer employed solely as a worker, just as if he were in a factory. Such a changeover may be long in coming, however, for the Korean farmers have not been easy to coerce. The few concessions made to them so far, such as the allowance for home gardens, indicate that the farmers are not following Communist procedures too enthusiastically, and that material—as opposed to Communist "spiritual"—incentives are required to insure production in the cooperatives.

According to official accounts, agricultural production has increased every year since the Korean War, except for 1959, when climatic conditions were bad. Rice, corn, potatoes, wheat, barley and millet are the leading crops. Rice comprises almost half the tonnages of production. Production of food grains, according to a speech by Kim Ilsung, was 3,803,000 tons in 1960, an increase of 32 percent over 1956. He confidently expected an additional million-ton production in 1961, and said that "we have now solved basically the food problem, one of the most difficult problems in the economic construction in our country."

Under the seven-year plan starting in 1960, mechanization of agriculture was to have a high priority. The number of tractors was to be increased from 13,000 in 1960, to 80,000 in 1967. Each county was to have its tractor station. New farm lands were to be opened up. Irrigation was to be increased so that grain production would increase to a level of 6,000,000 to 7,000,000 tons a year. In Kim Ilsung's words "the solution of the grain problem is one of the most cardinal tasks in socialist construction." It would appear that the problem is not yet completely solved, for North Korea has been purchasing some food grains from Australia. The seven-year plan calls also for an increased emphasis upon meat and fish production through large-scale stock farming and offshore fishing. It plans for great advances in housing for farm families by the erection of some 600,000 new homes and for the construction of many miles of roads in rural areas.

Industrial and Urban Development

The change in the agricultural sector of the economy has been more than equalled in industry and commerce under the Communist regime. For example, the current seven-year plan—in line with orthodox Marxist-Leninist economic theory—gives its greatest emphasis to the development of industries and the growth of cities.

Compared to South Korea, North Korea is rich in natural resources which can contribute to industrial development. This fact was recognized by the Japanese, who invested heavily in the discovery and exploitation of the mineral, forest and hydroelectric power resources of the northern part of the peninsula. At the end of World War II these activities came to a standstill. Dissolution was encouraged by the policy of the Russians at that time. Declaring North Korean resources and factory equipment as war booty, they took what they desired from the plants and stock piles, just as they were doing with Chinese industrial resources in Manchuria. However, as the Russians became more firmly established in North Korea and anxious to build up their puppet regime, industrial equipment began to be brought in from the Soviet Union and Eastern Europe.

The North Korean regime nationalized all industries. Two successive one-year plans, followed by a two-year plan, emphasized a military build-up. Technical supplies for the armed forces—tanks, trucks, planes—were imported largely from the Soviet Union. During the early days of the Korean War the DPRK troops, thus equipped, were very successful. As the front moved north of the 38th parallel, however, and as aerial and naval bombardment focused on the northern cities and industrial plants, the North suffered tremendous losses, not only in equipment and industrial facilities but in manpower. Thus at the end of the Korean War, North Korea had little industrial capacity and its trained labor force was decimated. The Soviet Union and its satellites aided in rehabilitation by providing new equipment. Little help came from Communist China, which was trying to develop its own industrial economy.

The DPRK launched a three-year plan in 1954–1956, a five-year plan from 1957–1961, and now are involved in a seven-year plan extending to 1967. The first three-year plan emphasized the coal and iron and steel industries as the basis for future development. The following five-year plan continued along these lines but devoted attention to machine tools, farm implements, mining machinery and chemical industries as well. In both plans reconstruction and development of the hydroelectric power plants were given high priority. The current seven-year plan provides for stand-by thermal power plants to be built to supplement the still expanding hydroelectric facilities and to furnish power throughout the year. In the first two plans not much emphasis was given to light

133

industry, but the present seven-year plan encourages the manufacture of textiles, home appliances, and footwear.

Along with industry the DPRK is attempting to rehabilitate the cities. New streets and municipal buildings have been laid out and public and educational facilities promoted. New apartments are to be built to house the increasing urban populations—living arrangements which are, of course, quite foreign to Korean culture. This is a part of a total pattern to refashion the Korean way of life and to provide effective control over the populace. The seven-year plan calls for another 600,000 apartment units to be built in the cities and their new suburbs and for the construction of "new and cozy houses for 600,000 families" in the rural areas.

It is hard to judge the effectiveness of these various plans for industrial and urban development. The very glowing reports and speeches from North Korea cannot be taken literally. But from the reports of outside observers who have traveled in North Korea there is no doubt but that considerable advances have been made. One of the major contributing factors has been the large amounts of foreign aid received from the Soviet Union and from its East European satellites. This aid tapered off in the late 1950's. Recently, as Sino-Soviet hostility, and hence Soviet-North Korean hostility, has grown, Communist China has increased its economic support. Another important factor has been the successful regimentation of the people.

A popular movement was fostered to whip up enthusiasm among the workers and to give recognition and benefits to the diligent. A symbol was chosen, that of a flying horse which according to ancient legends could leap a thousand *ri* (or three hundred miles) in a stride. Korean Communist leaders developed this indigenous "Flying Horse Movement" to parallel the "Great Leap Forward" of the Chinese. It would appear that the Korean effort has been relatively more successful,

134

partly because it was easier to organize 10,000,000 Korean people than 700,000,000 Chinese. Much of the work under the Flying Horse Movement was done by volunteer and extra labor from the agricultural teams and factory brigades into which the mass of the people were grouped. It was started as a part of the five-year plan which began in 1957 and has continued as a propaganda device of fluctuating effectiveness.

Cultural Development

The Flying Horse Movement is indicative of the emphasis which the DPRK places upon "spiritual" rather than material incentives for increasing economic production. One aim was certainly the further regimentation of the people. In the words of Kim Ilsung: "The Flying Horse Movement is very significant not only because it is a strong impetus to rapid economic development, but also because it is a wonderful popular and instructive medium for the reform of people into the new Communist personality." Through movements such as this, through both formal and informal education, and through the media of mass communication, the Communist regime has sought to remake the Korean people. Only time will tell how successful this has been.

Though it is a part of international communism the DPRK shows interesting nationalistic tendencies. In 1955, Kim Ilsung adopted a concept of national individuality or *chuche*. This was explained in his address to the Fourth Congress of the Korean Workers' Party in 1961, in words somewhat similar to those of Chinese Communist leaders: "By *chuche* we mean that in carrying out our revolution and construction we should creatively apply the general truth of Marxism-Leninism to the specific realities of our own country, and precisely and fully take into account our own historical and actual situation, our own capacity and the traditions, requirements and the level of the consciousness of our own people."

This emphasis on "our own" Korean history and traditions is evident in many cultural activities. There has been a revival of interest in old literature, folk songs, dances, and customs. Though often quite counter to modern Communist ideology, these cultural expressions can be adjusted to fit them to the Communist line or at least not have them deviate too greatly from it. The North Koreans apparently wish to keep Korea as an entity in the ideological struggle between the Soviet Union and Communist China. The cultural efforts are aimed at giving pride to a people who were long subjected to the Japanese, who have been under Russian occupation, and who were subjected to great shocks of defeat during the Korean War. Emphasis on the past and the renewal of folk dances and customs have provided both emotional outlets to a people whose traditional family structure has been broken down and a means of identifying the present Communist regime with the Korean past.

Naturally in seeking to develop the new Communist Korean personality the regime uses education as a prime moving force. After the Korean War schools were reconstructed and many teachers trained. It was necessary to send some able young people abroad for advanced education in the early years. Recently institutions of higher education, such as Kim Ilsung University in Pyongyang, have been opened. It is reported that universal primary education through the first nine years will be required by the end of the seven-year plan in 1967. Great emphasis has been put upon technical training. "Factory colleges" have been developed for part-time education. Adult education of various kinds including indoctrination in Communist ideology has been stressed. Newspapers, magazines and radio are widely used in the process. Thus, agricultural teams have "news reading meetings" at breaks in their workday. Women's and youth associations have classes for literacy training, complete with ideological orientation.

The emphasis upon education—a fourth of the North Korean people are now formally enrolled in some kind of school—is, of course, in line with the old traditional Korean respect and love for education. Now, however, it has been given Communist emphasis.

There can be no doubt that the life and character of North Korea has been changed during the years it has been under Communist control. The traditional ways of life, the economy, the family structure, and the society have been altered almost beyond recognition. Today, North Korea has a large and well-trained military force which is poised on the Truce Line. Its political structure is under the complete control of the North Korean Communist party (the Korean Workers' Party) led by dictatorial leader, Kim Ilsung, who consciously models himself along the lines of his close Chinese neighbor, Mao Tse-tung. The regime has increasingly followed the lead of the Chinese Communists, who rescued it from defeat in the Korean War. Periodically the 12,000,000 people of North Korea are whipped into excitement to rescue their fellow-countrymen from "the rapacious grasp of the American imperialists and their lackeys" in the south. Though they are reminded often of their past glories as a part of a Korean nationalistic fervor, their overlords are molding them more and more into a regimented Communist state through strict control of education and the media of communication. An economy and a society are being built where the independent individuality, long a characteristic of the North Korean "tiger hunters," is being systematically wiped out. The results are tragic for them and must be viewed with sorrow by anyone who hopes for "a unified, democratic and free Korea."

X. Regions of South Korea

The people of the Republic of Korea (ROK) have had severe trials and testings in the decades since their liberation from the Japanese in 1945. The development of a democratic and free society has been gradual and halting; it still is far from accomplishment. Though the people of South Korea have greatly desired a unification with their northern brothers, they are not willing to pay the price of subjugation to a Communist regime to achieve it. The ROK has been recognized by nations of the Free World as the only legitimate government in Korea and it holds membership in some of the United Nations agencies. Unfortunately, it is constantly under the menacing threat of a renewal of the Korean War.

Still lacking internal political stability, the ROK has to cope with complex and serious economic and social problems. From 1948 to 1960, Syngman Rhee controlled the government under an increasingly despotic regime. After his overthrow, a regime dedicated to more democratic principles was instituted. This, however, lasted less than a year and was replaced by an army-led regime. Elections held in 1963 continued the power of this military group, though now clothed in civilian attire. A population explosion, caused by rising birth rates and lowering death rates and an influx of refugees from North Korea, has practically negated the positive gains of increased productivity. The wavering economy of the ROK, unbalanced by the constant outlay for military purposes, had to be supported by massive infusions of American assistance, without which the country would have collapsed.

The volatile, freedom-loving people of South Korea have high aspirations for educational and cultural advancement. They are restive under restrictive regimes, particularly when these are marked by graft and corruption and by denial of individual freedoms. They desire to keep the best features of their traditional way of life and yet want to move quickly into a modern society. Strains and stresses, therefore, characterize South Korea today. Yet the "earth abides." The quiet beauty of the hills and valleys provides strength and surcease to the troubled Korean people.

Geographic Character

South Korea contains no such sharp geographic differences as does North Korea. It is more peninsular and maritime than the land to the north. The plains in the south are relatively extensive. The climate in winter is milder, so that two crops may be raised on many fields. As a consequence of these and other factors, the population of South Korea, 26,300,000 in 1963, is two and a half times that of North Korea. Yet the area comprises 38,000 square miles (as contrasted to 47,000 square miles of the north). These can be roughly divided into five geographic regions and two islands.

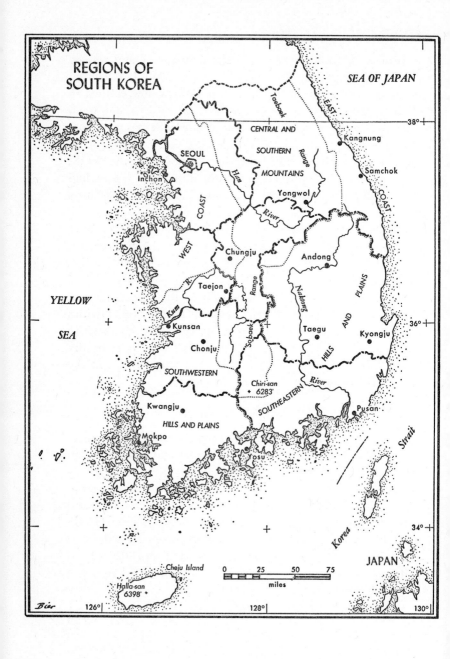

REGIONS OF SOUTH KOREA

SEA OF JAPAN

YELLOW SEA

CENTRAL AND SOUTHERN MOUNTAINS

Taebaek Range

SEOUL

Inchon

Han River

WEST COAST

Yongwol

Kangnung

Samchok

EAST COAST

Chungju

Andong

Taejon

Sobaek Range

Kum

Kunsan

Chonju

SOUTHWESTERN

HILLS AND PLAINS

Kwangju

Mokpo

Yosu

Chiri-san + 6283'

Naktong River

Taegu

HILLS AND PLAINS

Kyongju

SOUTHEASTERN

Pusan

Korea Strait

JAPAN

Cheju Island

Halla-san 6398' +

0   25   50   75
miles

Bier

126°   128°   130°

38°

36°

34°

The East Coast

The Taebaek range extending north and south and forming the spine of mid-Korea effectively isolates a narrow littoral along the east coast. This range also acts as a climatic barrier, for the warm ocean current which flows northward along the coast gives to this region relatively mild winter temperatures. The small river valleys are separated by headlands which differ in their geologic character. In some areas resistant slate and other metamorphic rocks give a sharp angularity to the landscape; in others, easily eroded biotite granites have resulted in rolling hills.

The East Coast, some 2,000 square miles in area, is not a closely knit region. The Japanese started to build a rail line along the coast but this was never put into operation. A highway extends the length of the region and a few roads lead westward across the Taebaek range. Though at one time a local kingdom controlled the region it was absorbed into Silla over a thousand years ago. Politically the East Coast is a backward part of Kangwon province, yet county borders coinciding with the drainage divide give the region some political separateness.

Most of the 600,000 people who live in the region are farmers, cultivating rice and cereals in small fields in the pocket-like valleys, gathering firewood and cutting lumber in the hills. The winter temperatures average a little below freezing, 31.5° Fahrenheit in the south and four degrees colder in the north. The rainfall, concentrated in the summer months, averages forty to fifty inches a year. Spring rains, though not large in amount, fortuitously come at a crucial time for rice transplanting. Because of the mild winter temperatures barley is a common crop and may even be planted in some of the well-drained paddy fields. Most of the agricultural production

141

is used for local consumption making the region comparatively self-sufficient for food.

Fishing along the coast is a major enterprise, concentrated since the Japanese era in a few ports where motorized boats and modern nets can be docked.

In the southern part of the region, at Samchok, coal resources in the nearby mountain areas furnish an economic base for cement and chemical industries. Most of the industry within the region, however, has been confined to simple home handicrafts; these are declining, as mass-produced articles are introduced into the markets. Centrally located Kangnung is the leading commercial town. Like most of the towns in the region, it is set back from the coast a few miles—a location which goes back to the days when the coastal region was plagued by Japanese pirates.

The East Coast has great natural beauty, particularly in the north, where the mountains extend close down to the shore. Tourist facilities have been developed to exploit this resource. Most of the region, though not spectacularly beautiful, has the charm of a simple rural landscape. Along the roads leading to the villages of thatch-roofed houses are small shrines dedicated to the memory of some illustrious ancestors. In spots that afford an especially picturesque view, scholars in past centuries gathered in pavilions for poetry composing and reading. Unfortunately, many of these pavilions now are tumbled down; modern life provides little leisure for the scholarly contemplation and companionship of the old days.

Though the fighting during the Korean War caused no great damage in the East Coast region, it was affected, as was all of Korea, by the tragedies of the war. Refugees crowded into the villages, young men were conscripted for military service, troops were trained or quartered in hastily built encampments. An airfield was built near Kangnung and the strategic roads were improved, particularly the major highways that led over the mountains to the west. The East Coast is changing rapidly from its former isolated and self-sufficient economy and society, but it will long be a distinctive region geographically.

The Central and Southern Mountains

The Taebaek range and its offshoot to the southwest, the Sobaek range, form the major drainage divides of South Korea. These ranges and the hill regions which border them make up another distinctive region in South Korea, though its exact boundaries are difficult to delineate. In this mountain and hill region population is concentrated in the river valleys, at mining and logging camps, or along the rail lines which traverse the region. It is estimated that in the 13,000 square miles that make up this region, the largest in South Korea, there are roughly 3,500,000 people. There are no large cities but numerous market and administrative towns and hundreds of villages.

The Korean War and the subsequent "digging in" along the Truce Line have profoundly changed the northern part of the region. Front line defenses utilize the rugged terrain. Military support installations, airfields and supply depots back up the front. However, the rest of the region was not so affected by the Korean War, except for some mountainous areas where North Korean troops, cut off from retreat, attempted to carry on guerrilla warfare.

The mountains and hills act as a barrier between the western and eastern plains in central Korea. Though not so sharp or rugged as the mountainous Northern Interior in North Korea, the profusion of hills and mountains creates transportation difficulties. Geologically the region is made up of a complex of granite and metamorphosed rocks, whose structure has a general trend northeast and southwest. The whole central block was leveled to a rolling plain in relatively recent

143

geologic time and then tilted upward, with the crest paralleling the east coast. Into this block the west flowing rivers were entrenched in great loops and tributary streams etched their way back into the higher elevations of the upthrown block. To the south there was a slightly different geologic history. There was less of a tilting of the structure and more of a massive rise. The results similarly produced a maze of mountains and hills with narrow river valleys.

The variation in elevation accounts for considerable differences in temperature range and in natural vegetation. In the few areas above 6,000 feet, alpine flora may be found, reflecting the cold winter and cool summer temperatures. In the elevations between 3,000 and 6,000 feet which make up most of the region there are mixed hardwoods and conifers. Here, as in so many other wooded regions, the inroads made by wood-seeking farmers or insect blights have denuded much of the land of its virgin forests. Second growths of scrub oak and deformed pines clothe much of the region, but now great efforts are being expended on reforestation and protection of the forest lands. Some day, decades from now, the forest resources of the region may be of great significance, not only for lumber but for protection from the flooding of the rivers which originate in these mountains. The heavy rainfall of forty-five to fifty-five inches, concentrated in the summer months, comes with rapid runoff. It could be much more beneficial than is now the case if reforestation projects could be greatly expanded.

Self-sufficient agriculture is the occupation of most of the population in the Central and Southern Mountains. Most of the farmers live in small villages located along the edges of the river valleys. They produce rice on small paddy fields developed on the river flood plains and cereals such as barley, soybeans, and vegetables on dry fields on the lower hill slopes. Some farmers live dispersed among the remote mountains

144

growing cereals such as millet, buckwheat and rye under hardy conditions. Many of the farmers are part-time wood gatherers as well and supply firewood and lumber to the densely populated regions and large cities bordering the region.

As the population of Korea increased under the Japanese settlement began to penetrate this region. Fields were cleared on the hill slopes, and simple irrigation systems installed to provide water for paddy fields on the flood plains. Of particular importance was the construction of roads which tapped the forest lands. Railroads were built across the mountains in order to provide routes between Pusan in the southeast and Seoul. The main line went over a pass at the narrowest part of the region. Another rail line built more recently went north from Pusan, through Andong, and then across to the drainage basin of the Han River and into Seoul from the east.

From this second rail line a branch was built to the east leading to the Yongwol coal fields, whose deposits of a low-grade anthracite are the major coal resources of South Korea. Greatly expanded in recent years, they have permitted the construction of several cement and chemical industries and a large thermal power plant. Scattered deposits of gold, graphite, tungsten and numerous minor metals in the Central and Southern Mountains have turned out to be of minor importance because of their limited size and their remoteness, making them costly to develop. In the upper reaches of the Han River, dams have been built for hydroelectric power production, but these are small in capacity compared to the plants in North Korea.

The Central and Southern Mountains are not an inviting region, yet many people, pushed by the population pressures, are trying to gain a living there from the inhospitable land. Farmers must work hard to grow crops on the limited agricultural lands along the river valleys. People are isolated and provincial in their outlook. During the Korean War they had to provide for the many refugees who poured into the region but these transients could not remain in an area of such limited resources. Many of the towns were badly damaged by aerial bombardment and by the street fighting that took place as the tides of war washed back and forth across them. New military roads and installations have completely modified some of the northern parts of the region. In the south, many of the villages still remain in their quiet isolation, and high in the forested mountains Buddhist monasteries are tucked away where time seemingly stands still.

The West Coast

The West Coast of South Korea is dominated by the city of Seoul. With a population over 3,000,000, it furnishes a large market for food and firewood that are supplied from the outlying area. Many people work in the city and its industrial suburbs, but keep their families in the countryside. All roads lead into the city and Seoul puts a particular stamp upon the region of the West Coast.

This region is composed of broad valleys and numerous islands. The down-thrown portion of the large crustal block that makes up central Korea extends out under the shallow Yellow Sea. On this block have been deposited alluvial materials brought down from the Central Mountains by the Han River and other streams. Above the plains are some hills of more resistant material, parts of old earth folds which make up the base of the crustal block. Alluvial materials lap around these hills like the sea about small islands.

The hills provide a firm base for the villages and towns, protecting them somewhat from the cold blasts of winter. January temperatures average 22° Fahrenheit at Seoul and are only a few degrees above that in the southern part of the region. Precipitation in the form of snow is limited in the

146

winter months. Less than eight inches of the annual average rainfall of fifty inches at Seoul come during the winter half of the year. In the summer the temperatures are high, in the seventies, and heavy rainfall compounds the discomfort.

This region is a densely populated one. In an area comprising 6,000 square miles there are, in addition to the 3,000,000 people concentrated in Seoul itself, another 5,000,000 in the surrounding areas. The land is intensively cultivated. The barren hills reflect the intensity with which the forests have been cut to provide firewood. Fortunately, the alluvial soils on the plains, including the areas reclaimed from the shallow sea, produce excellent crops if they are irrigated, well drained, and adequately fertilized. Rice is the favored crop, but on the hill slopes or where the soils are too sandy to hold water, dry crops such as barley and other cereals are grown. Because of the large urban market, vegetables are intensively cultivated. Some fishing is done in the rivers and in the Yellow Sea, though there is not an abundant supply.

The word Seoul means "the capital." Since it was made the capital of the Yi dynasty shortly after 1392, the city has been the center of the Korean peninsula. It is set in a natural amphitheatre of hills, along the crest of which ran a stone wall pierced by eight gates. Some of these gates are still preserved, though the wall has largely disappeared. (Its stones made excellent foundation rocks for houses.) Seoul has had a tremendous growth with the modernization of Korea. The Japanese took over the old palaces of the Yi dynasty and preserved some of the palace grounds as public parks. They built an imposing white stone building to house their Government-General. Today it is the seat of the ROK government. Fifty years ago Seoul was a city made up of block after block of one-story houses separated by twisting alleys. The modern city boasts a number of ten- and fifteen-story buildings and a grid pattern of major streets. Some of the more durable

147

structures are those of Christian churches, whose steeples pierce the sky line. A stream, which in olden times flowed through the city and helped divide it into districts, has recently been covered over and used for a roadway. Other new streets have been cut through the city and a streetcar and bus system furnishes public transportation.

In recent decades Seoul has spread far beyond its original walls, mainly southward to and across the Han River. Some of the suburbs are residential. Some are industrial with new factories for the processing and production of consumer goods. Other suburbs are mainly commercial, especially along the railroads which come into Seoul from every direction. For defensive purposes many military installations have been built within and around the capital city. Thirty-five miles to the east is the seaport of Inchon which was increased greatly in size as an industrial and shipping center. The area between Seoul and Inchon is being built up with new factories.

Seoul is not only the political and commercial center of Korea, it is also the cultural center. For example, there are some thirty-five colleges and universities in the city and its suburbs. The city of Seoul teems with life. Old palaces and traditional market places still exist, but most of the city is modern with buses and cars and countless bicycles, motorcycles, and carts on busy streets and with crowds of people hurrying along the sidewalks and shopping in modern stores.

During the Korean War Seoul was alternately lost and regained, lost and regained, yet the effects of devastation have largely disappeared. Most of the rubble has been cleaned away. New roads and buildings replace the ruins caused by the war. The influx of refugees from North Korea has created quite a profound change, for many of these people settled down in Seoul. Many have become leaders within the city. Some sections are made up almost exclusively of people from the north, all of them longing to return to their native places.

148

The addition of these hundreds of thousands, plus the many rural Koreans who have been attracted to urban life and its economic and educational opportunities, has resulted in a great, swollen city with serious problems of urban development.

The Southwestern Hills and Plains

The region most favored for agriculture in Korea is the southwest. Here alluvial plains, broad river valleys, low hill slopes, and a propitious climate combine to give good conditions for cultivation of rice, the favored crop of all Korean farmers. The Japanese stimulated production of rice for export. The relatively mild winters are suited to the cultivation of a second crop, usually barley. Thus, it is in this region of 7,000,000 people and 7,500 square miles that the densest rural populations are found in Korea. There is no large metropolis, but many ports and towns that provide economic and political services to the hundreds of villages. Traditional ways of life have a very strong hold on the people despite the impact of recent history and introduction of modern technology. Not greatly damaged by the Korean War, it is the agricultural heartland of the Republic of Korea.

In the northern part of the region the Kum River and its tributaries form the largest plain in Korea. On these relatively flat alluvial lands and adjoining areas reclaimed from tidal flats the Japanese developed extensive irrigation facilities. Reservoirs were built in the hill lands bordering the plains. Water was led in a network of straight canals out on the plains. High quality seed and transplanting in strictly measured rows increased production of rice. In some areas heavy use of commercial fertilizers, also, resulted in large yields. Much of this rice did not go into Korean kitchens but was exported through the port of Kunsan to Japan.

In the southern part of the region the geologic structural

149

lines go at cross angles and form a maze of hills, valleys and islands along the coast. The extensions of the Sobaek range culminate at massive Chiri-san on the borders of the region. The interior valleys, formed by structural down-faulting and covered with a veneer of alluvial materials, are fertile and can be easily irrigated by simple gravity water systems flowing from ponds in the hills. Along the crenulated coast, made up of numerous islands and peninsulas, there are small plains often at the heads of bays. Even here there is intensive cultivation.

The climate of the Southwestern Hills and Plains so well suited to rice production has an average annual rainfall varying from forty-five to sixty inches, with the spring rains usually coming opportunely at the time of rice transplanting. Heavy rains in the hot summer, when monthly temperatures average 80°, keep the paddy fields covered with water. Dry weather in the fall enables the rice to be more easily cut and dried. Then in the mild winters when average monthly temperatures are around 32° many of the paddy fields may be planted to a crop of barley.

In order to develop this region and change it from its self-sufficient agricultural economy to a commercial rice exporting region, the Japanese developed a system of roads, railroads, milling and warehouse centers, and ports. Taejon was a completely new city built at a junction of the main Pusan-Seoul rail line. Another rail line extended southwest from Taejon, past Iri, another new town, to the port of Mokpo with branch lines going westward to Kunsan and southward to the port of Yosu. Taejon was the scene of bitter fighting during the Korean War, but has been rebuilt since 1952, much as it was before, in a modern style with a grid pattern of streets and many warehouses and factories. Some of the old towns, such as Kwangju and Chonju, also have had considerable population growth as textile factories, rice mills, and various consumer-goods manufacturing plants were built in their suburbs.

Along with the commercialization of agriculture there was also under the Japanese a very rapid growth of rural tenancy in this region. However, in 1949 a land reform system was instituted which gave ownership of the land back to the farmers. In many respects this resulted in less efficient operations, for the holdings were small and not operated on an economic scale. Moreover, short-term systems of payment, unrealistic government control over prices for farm produce, rampant inflation, and upsetting of the normal economy by the Korean War served to offset advantages that might have come from the land reform. Many of the former tenant farmers found themselves owning small plots of land but unable to make a satisfactory living from them. Thus, an area which had been able in the past to produce great amounts of rice for export to the cities of Korea and abroad, has not been playing a very effective role in the economy. Large imports of commercial fertilizer under American aid programs have helped keep up production, but much more could be done to stabilize the agricultural economy and increase the agricultural production so that once again the Southwestern Hills and Plains could be Korea's rice bowl.

Southeastern Hills and Valleys

The Naktong River drains a large basin in Southeastern Korea. This region of hills and valleys has long been densely populated. It was the site of the Silla dynasty, which ruled most of the Korean peninsula from 668 to 935 A.D. The region comprises Kyongsang province divided into a northern and a southern section by the Japanese. Here the people still speak Korean with a distinctive dialect and accent. Facing toward Japan, the area has been considerably influenced by the Japanese. The port of Pusan, built by the Japanese, is the

151

third largest city in Korea after Seoul and Pyongyang. Another large city is Taegu, centrally located along the Naktong. This is not only a political and commercial center but also the location of many industrial plants processing consumer goods such as textiles and cigarettes.

The Naktong River and its tributaries are entrenched in great loops in a structural basin made up mainly of sedimentary strata, warped and faulted in past geologic time. Along the river valleys are fertile alluvial plains. Most of the countryside is marked by low hills, except for mountainous areas adjoining the Central and Southern Mountains which block Southeastern Korea off from the rest of the peninsula. The region comprises an area of 10,800 square miles and has a population of 9,000,000.

Because of its southern location and the warm currents which flow from the south through the Korea Straits, the Southeastern Hills and Valleys have mild winters. January temperatures along the coast average just above freezing; inland the January temperatures average three or four degrees colder. These inland areas also have the hottest summers in Korea, averaging above 80°. As in all of Korea the rainfall, which averages forty inches a year, is at a peak in the summer months, when it averages twenty-five inches. Occasional typhoons in the early fall may bring heavy rainfall and destructive winds.

Like Southwestern Korea, this region is well suited to the production of rice. There are no extensive plains but the numerous river valleys can be irrigated and the lower hill slopes can be terraced. These fields are used for the intensive cultivation of rice in the summer and of barley in the winter. Double cropping is more common here than elsewhere in Korea. Agricultural crops are also diversified, with native cotton, soybeans, and tobacco grown on dry fields during the summer. Some of the fields on the hill slopes are also devoted to mulberry for silkworm feeding and to fruit orchards, such as apples, pears and persimmons.

In addition to the two large cities there are numerous towns and hundreds of villages, well linked by railroads and highways. The former capital of the Silla dynasty, Kyongju, has many old-style, tiled roofed homes of the yangban class. The grave mounds, some of which have been excavated to yield old treasures, and the Buddhist temples in the vicinity have made the Kyongju area an attraction for tourists. Throughout the region among the thatched roofed villages, the tiled roofs of the landlords' homes stand out. The inhabitants of the Southeastern Hills and Valleys are marked by their conservatism. Local loyalties are very deep. Buddhism has had a continuing, profound influence since the days of the Silla dynasty.

This region was severely affected by the Korean War. Throngs of refugees were crowded into the Pusan perimeter. The hills around Pusan were covered by packing-box shacks which too often went up in flames. The wharves and warehouses of Pusan, so essential in supplying the UN Forces during the Korean War, is still Korea's major commercial port.

Pusan and other ports along the island-fringed coast are also used as the base for a fishing industry of increasing importance. The fishing waters offshore to a distance of as much as fifty miles are claimed by the Koreans. Japanese fishermen who used to fish in the area, marked off by the so-called Rhee Line, were resentful over this prohibition. Conflict frequently broke out as Korean coastal guards seized Japanese fishing boats. Despite this, there are still ties between Southeastern Korea and Japan; for example, Japanese radio stations and even TV stations are listened to and seen in Pusan. As the disagreements between Japan and Korea are resolved, Pusan may enjoy another economic upsurge, for it is the natural gateway to Korea from Japan.

153

Ullung Island

Out in the Sea of Japan, some eighty miles east off the East Coast of Korea, is small Ullung Island. Having an area of some thirty square miles and a population of 20,000 people, it is important mainly as a fishing base. Geologically, Ullung is a segment of the volcanic line which extends southward from Paek-tu-san on the north Korean boundary. Its rocky soils do not provide for much agriculture. The forests have some botanically interesting species and have been a source for shipbuilding timbers. Since Ullung is so different from the rest of Korea, it must be classed as a separate geographic region. Isolated as it is, it has only rare visitors and limited contact with the rest of South Korea.

Still farther away to the east are some rocky islets called Tokto in Korean, Takeshima in Japanese, and Liancourt Rocks on old British navigation charts. Around them are some seaweed beds and some fishing grounds, but they are of miniscule economic importance. However, the Rocks are claimed by both Japan and Korea and so have become an issue of national pride. The Koreans now base a handful of lonely guards on the hitherto uninhabited islets, for some Japanese took down the Korean flag in one recent episode. This irritating issue aggravated tension between Korea and Japan out of all proportion to the economic importance of the Rocks.

Cheju Island

Off the southwest coast some sixty miles is another volcanic island, Cheju. This is much larger than Ullung, comprising some 700 square miles and housing a population of 300,000 people. Its history has been distinctive. For many centuries the inhabitants lived under a form of matriarchy, for the women of this island, who engaged in seaweed collection and pearl diving, also held the economic power. In the Yi dynasty,

Cheju was used as a place of exile for politicians who had lost favor in the court at Seoul. In more recent times, it has been governed as a part of Cholla which is the political province of southwest Korea. Then in 1948 the ROK made it a separate political province. This was in partial recognition of its distinctive geographic character.

The core of the island is Halla-san, 6,450 feet in elevation, a symmetrically shaped volcanic mass which was last active in 1007 A.D. The lava flows stretching down from the summit are covered with rocks and ash. The rainfall, averaging fifty-five inches a year, soaks into the volcanic soil so there are no permanent streams. Only a few small patches of alluvial material are fertile; most of the fields on the lower slopes are devoted to hardy dry crops: millet, barley, buckwheat, and sweet potatoes, with relatively low yields. The once luxuriant forests on the higher slopes have been mostly cut off. In their place are scrub, second growth forests, and in some areas grasslands which can be used for grazing. Cheju is the only area of Korea where animal husbandry is an important part of the economy. Centuries ago, particularly during the period of Mongol influence in Korea, horses were pastured on the grassy slopes. These sturdy small pack ponies were exported to the mainland. In recent decades cattle and goats have been introduced on these grasslands.

The fishing industry, including the traditional seaweed, shellfish and pearl oyster gathering, still employs women and is of major importance in the economy of Cheju. With the restrictions placed upon Japanese fishermen by the Rhee line, Korean fishermen based on Cheju and on ports on the adjacent mainland were able to get good catches in these fishing waters.

Cheju might have had great significance during the Korean War if the Pusan perimeter had fallen to the Communist advance. During the Korean War there was a great influx of

155

refugees, but most of them longed to return to the mainland, for they found the landscape of Cheju strange to their eyes. For example, rice fields are lacking, the walls of the houses are made of volcanic rocks, the thatched roofs extend far out over the eaves in order to catch water for household use, stone fences separate fields and protect farm yards. However, Cheju did not become a Korean Formosa and it has now settled back into its role as a distinctive and picturesque part of Korea.

XI. *The Republic of Korea*

The American troops coming into Korea to accept the surrender of the Japanese on September 8, 1945, were faced with a difficult situation for which they had been little prepared. Korea, a hitherto unified land, had been split by the 38th parallel. The Korean people, long under Japanese domination, had little concept of or training for a free and democratic government. The Korean economy geared to the Japanese war effort, controlled by Japanese managerial personnel, and with a massive government financial involvement, had to be reoriented and reorganized. Particularly, there was a paucity of skilled workers and managers, though there were many Korean businessmen eager to grasp ownership and make quick profits. Politicians quickly appeared on the scene and formed myriad parties, grouped into shifting coalitions; many were interested chiefly in personal aggrandizement and power. South Korea plunged into a turbulent period of its history and the country has not yet reached stability.

157

United States Military Government

American military authorities, ignoring the People's Committees which had been hastily formed by Korean groups, operated for three years a military government with varying degrees of success. During this time attempts were made to encourage Korean political leadership, but the Interim Assembly, half of whose members were appointed, was not very effective. The local government was labeled "an interpreter's government," for persons with a knowledge of English seemed to be preferred for high positions. In December, 1945, a four-power meeting in Moscow agreed to set up a Joint Commission to achieve a unification of Korea. However, the Commission meeting in Seoul in the spring of 1946, and again in the spring of 1947, was bogged down by the Russian insistence that consultations would only be held with those Korean groups who were not opposed to them.

On September 23, 1947, the United States presented the Korean problem to the United Nations General Assembly. The UN Temporary Commission was not allowed to operate in North Korea, but did oversee elections on May 10, 1948 in South Korea. The elections were considered by the UN Commission to be "a valid expression of the free will of the electorate." The elected Assembly then worked out a constitution for the Republic of Korea (ROK) and organized a government, to be headed by Syngman Rhee. The reins of power were handed to this government by General Douglas MacArthur on August 15, 1948. The United Nations General Assembly on December 12, 1948, resolved that this was "a lawful government" and "the only such government in Korea."

Syngman Rhee's Republic

The ROK was organized in an American pattern with executive, legislative, and judicial branches. In actual fact, the judicial was often subservient to the executive branch, and there was a constant friction between the legislative and executive branches. Generally the executive branch, headed by President Rhee, emerged in times of crisis with the real power. Rhee forced through a number of constitutional changes in the next few years that further strengthened his presidential powers, though he made a show of preserving democratic processes and organizations.

Syngman Rhee was a complex individual. As a young man he had been involved in attempts to liberalize the government under the Korean monarchy in the late 1890's. After a period in prison, when he was subjected to torture, he escaped to Japan and eventually to Hawaii and the United States. (Throughout his life one of his common gestures was stroking the knuckles of his fingers which had been deformed by the tortures.) He studied in colleges in the United States, taking graduate work under Woodrow Wilson at Princeton. He returned to Korea for YMCA work, but finally left for Hawaii in 1912, after the Japanese had taken over Korea.

As an exile, Rhee was involved in the long struggle for independence for Korea. The exile groups were split by factionalism and Rhee was the opinionated leader of one of the factions. In the late 1930's and during World War II, Rhee served as the Washington representative of the conservative government-in-exile, based in China, though he often acted very much on his own. Over the age of seventy, Rhee returned to Korea in 1945 accompanied by his wife, an Austrian whom he had met in Europe when he was pleading the cause of Korean independence at the League of Nations.

President Rhee was an adroit and somewhat ruthless politician. Whenever any opposition leader became too strong or even when some of his own followers showed signs of excessive popular strength, he moved to destroy them—and was usually successful. Sometimes his followers resorted to

159

assassination to keep the opposition in line and even staged assassination attempts on their own leaders to gain popular support for harsh measures which suppressed human liberties and democratic action. As Rhee passed into his eighties he became more and more divorced from the political needs of the country. A small clique of individuals surrounded him and used his prestige for their own graft, corruption, and power.

Yet, despite his faults, Syngman Rhee played a major role during the Korean War. He was resilient in these times of adversity and served as a rallying point for the Korean people. He had a deep-seated hatred for the Japanese, against whom he had fought for over thirty years in exile. He was volatile in character, reversing his friendships and displaying his anger, particularly if he felt that outsiders were interfering with his ideas. Above all, he was consistently anti-Communist and often classed all persons who were more liberal minded than he as Communists or fellow travelers.

From 1948 to 1960 the ROK was a "strong man" government. An opposition existed but it was ineffectual and offered little political alternative to the Korean people. The ever-present police and youth corps were often called upon to suppress nascent anti-Rhee movements. However, in the election of 1956, which was observed by UN teams, Rhee's running mate was defeated for the vice-presidency by a former Rhee supporter who had broken with him, John M. Chang, a Catholic layman. In the legislative assembly elections in 1958, the opposition Democrat Party and independents won seats at the expense of the official candidates of Rhee's Liberal Party. (Actually, party labels had little real meaning; neither party was democratic or liberal; both were coalitions of conservative personalities.) Korean military officers began to play more of a political role, particularly after the Korean War. The army leaders were well trained; they had been tested by war. Many of the military disapproved of the excessive personal graft and corruption of some of the civilian officials, particularly when it deprived the military forces of supplies and funds. Also, the army opposed the police, who were still applying the harsh methods of control they had learned under the Japanese.

The elections held in the spring of 1960 served as a spark to ignite anti-Rhee feelings. Rhee (by now at least 85 years old) was running for a fourth term. The Liberal Party, wishing to assure his election, and also that of his running mate, went to extraordinary lengths to suppress opposition and rig the votes in rural areas. Some students who were supporting opposition candidates were subjected to police brutality; the bound body of one student was found floating in the harbor at a southern port. This brutality and the unbelievable sweeping election of the Rhee party brought the college and high school students of Seoul out in a protest march on April 19, 1960. The police shot down 125 of these students, provoking a violent reaction.

Martial law was imposed, but the rioting continued. The Korean Army sympathized with the rioters and army leaders expressed the view that a group of professors had "just demands" when they called for the resignation of key officials in all three branches of the government. If the army had come out strongly in favor of Rhee he probably would have weathered this crisis, but many segments of the army took pro-reform stands. Rhee and his party were doomed. The United States Government in a State Department note expressed its opposition to the harsh measures which had been used. This was a final blow. On April 27, Rhee resigned and two days later an aged broken man left with his wife for retirement in Hawaii.

161

John M. Chang's Republic

In July free elections took place and a new government headed by John M. Chang as Premier and Yun Posun as titular president took office. Unfortunately, the new government was marked by internal dissension; Chang never succeeded in obtaining a workable majority in the new legislative bodies. Graft and corruption continued. The discredited police, though reorganized, were unable to preserve law and order effectively. Several groups openly advocated some form of rapprochment with North Korea. Under a free press policy numerous newspapers, some of them only mimeographed leaflets, came into being; in many cases they served only for blackmailing purposes. Freedom of the press was not accompanied by responsibility. The nation's economy deteriorated: currency reforms were not successful in halting inflation and black markets flourished. The widely publicized agricultural improvement programs were slow in starting, and when unfavorable weather curtailed crops, the perennial "spring hunger" of the farming areas was severe indeed. Army leaders found their position threatened by projected cuts in military budgets.

The reaction to the situation was almost inevitable: A bloodless coup by military leaders took place on May 16, 1961. American officials in Korea attempted to preserve the Chang regime, but Washington officials appeared to condone the action of the military. John M. Chang and his cabinet went into hiding and in a few days gave themselves up to arrest on charges of corruption. President Yun Posun was kept in office to lend a semblance of legality to the government. A Supreme Council for National Reconstruction made up of thirty-two military officers took over the reins of government and proceeded to institute constitutional and administrative changes. The Commander-in-Chief of the Army

162

was the titular head of the Supreme Council, but after a few weeks he was forced to resign and the real power of the military junta emerged, Major General Park Chunghee.

The Military Junta Government

General Park, the strong man of the junta, was born in southeastern Korea. After a high school education he enlisted in the Japanese army where he underwent rigorous training. With the liberation of Korea Park joined the gendarmerie and advanced in rank quite rapidly, partly, no doubt, because of his previous military experience. As an ROK colonel in southeastern Korea, he was accused of being involved in a Communist-inspired revolt and was sentenced to death. He was, however, pardoned by President Rhee when the President was convinced by an American military observer that some intra-army politics were at work. Reinstated, Park served in the Korean War in various capacities, largely of a staff nature. He was one of the leaders in a group of younger officers who are reported to have discussed a coup even prior to the fall of Syngman Rhee. Junior in rank and age to many of the other original members of the junta, Park, with the assistance of other young officers, was able to manipulate the senior and better-known officers effectively until he and his followers were prepared to assume command. Park is an alert, trim and professional soldier with great personal ambition. He understands some English, but purposely speaks in Korean. Many South Korean political figures are Christians, but Park's religious background is Buddhist. Korean military commanders and political leaders have often undergone lengthy military and academic training in America, but he has not, nor has he been too closely associated with Americans. General Park is an independent thinker and, like Syngman Rhee, resents any real or implied direction by outsiders.

The Supreme Council in its early months promulgated laws

163

aimed at reforming the evils which they felt were undermining Korea. Particularly they assailed graft and corruption. Hoodlums and prostitutes were taken into custody. The multitude of irresponsible newspapers were suppressed. Koreans who had become rich through shady means were heavily fined or forced to make large donations to national economic projects. Political activities were suspended and political appointees were superseded in their positions, initially by military officers and later by some nonpolitical, technically-trained civilians. The junta promised that after a period of reform, estimated to be two years in length, and after the drawing up of a new constitution, elections would be held for a civilian government. This promise was applauded by the United States, which continued its massive, and vital, economic aid program.

After General Park had solidified his position, the Supreme Council found the governance of the ROK to be more complex than they had anticipated. They decreed a five-year economic plan aimed at revitalization and realistic growth of the economy, but it was slow in getting started. In the meantime, inflation, population pressures, and stagnation in some sectors of the economy made much of the plan ineffectual. The initial reforming zeal abated. The military officers found that a civilian economy and society cannot be changed by orders or decrees.

Park's chief lieutenant, Colonel Kim Chongpil, the head of the all-powerful Central Intelligence Agency, wished to organize a political party which would perpetuate General Park in power when civilian control was reinstituted. Requiring funds, Kim is reported to have started to accumulate a party purse of great magnitude. One method was to manipulate the stock market. So graft and corruption had not disappeared but had only changed their character and scope. However, the petty graft which had been so prevalent and irksome in Korea was curtailed, as were the black markets. Also, under the military political power one could observe a greater respect for law and order than during the chaotic times of the Chang regime when students and others felt free to parade and protest on every conceivable subject.

The junta issued a "White Paper" shortly after it came into power dealing with the emerging form of "Korean democracy." "The Korean people have no tradition of and no experience with real democracy," it stated. The junta government faced the task of creating "an atmosphere that will permit the emergence of true democracy in a form that will be workable against this background." After some months restrictions on political action were eased. Many thousands of Koreans who had been involved in political action in the past had their names put on a black list, and could be removed only by appeal. It was over this issue that President Yun Posun finally resigned. General Park replaced him as acting president. When it appeared that the elections promised for 1963 were to be indefinitely delayed, the United States Government, backed by other nations, exerted great pressure to have this decision reversed and elections held.

One of the major reasons that General Park hesitated to hold elections was that he was uncertain of his political strength. Scandals and conflicts among army groups had weakened the Democratic-Republican Party which Park's political lieutenant Kim Chongpil had formed. Kim had been forced to resign from his directorship of the Korean C.I.A. and had been sent abroad. Though for a time Park withdrew his candidacy for the presidency under pressure from certain army leaders, he was able ultimately to recover some of his political prestige and thus ran as the Democratic-Republican candidate in the election held on October 15, 1963. He was opposed by a number of candidates. One of them, General Song, a former Premier, was backed by a group of "moderate" colonels. The leading opposition candidate, however, was Yun Posun, the former President. Two other civilian candidates dropped out at the last minute. It is interesting to speculate what might have happened if the opposition groups had united to campaign for only one candidate, for General Park won over Yun by only 156,000 votes. The election was notably fair. Yun's major strength was in Seoul and in the northern rural areas; Park had strength in Pusan and in the southern rural areas.

These elections for the presidency were followed on November 26 by election for seats in the Parliament. Again, the opposition parties were greatly fragmented, generally backing individual candidates on the basis of family and sectional loyalties. General Park's Democratic-Republican Party, to which some of the "moderate" colonels had been admitted, won 110 out of the 175 seats. In actual votes, however, Park's party carried only one-third of the total. The fragmentation of the opposition groups led to their defeat.

The Republic of Park Chunghee

With his position as president assured and the subsequent victory of his Democratic-Republican Party in the Parliament, Park Chunghee found himself in a strong position. However, he had had to make concessions to military leaders and his narrow victory pointed up the strong opposition to him personally and to some of his closest colleagues, such as Kim Chongpil. To keep in power he would have to depend greatly on his regime's ability to meet the country's pressing economic problems. He needed American economic and military aid but was not always willing to take advice on ways that it could be used most effectively. Above all, he had to keep the military forces convinced of the effectiveness of his leadership in maintaining Korea's military strength and economic stability.

166

One of the problems facing the Park regime was to develop normal relations with Japan. This was particularly urged by the United States government. However, groups existed within Korea who opposed the normalization of diplomatic and economic relations. Businessmen feared competition from Japan. Students were particularly vocal in opposition, mirroring a somewhat illogical but real fear of a loss of independence. Nevertheless, the Park regime agreed to talks, which were usually held in Tokyo. Among the major issues were reparation payments, the ownership of assets in Japan, fishing rights in the Korea Straits and Sea of Japan, and legal status of Koreans in Japan. Finally in June 1965, a brief basic treaty between Japan and the ROK was signed, though some of the issues were not completely settled. It called for an exchange of envoys and confirmed that the ROK was "the only lawful government in Korea."

Another very real problem facing the Park regime was to encourage the Korean people to develop a better sense of participation and responsibility toward their government. For centuries the national government had been considered at the grass roots level as a remote instrumentality that oppressed the people with heavy taxes and onerous laws. This attitude strengthened during the decades of Japanese control. Though welcoming their freedom in 1945, the Korean people still did not sense the responsibility that was the essential guarantee of that freedom. The task of developing, on the basis of national pride, a trust and belief in national government remains today. There is still much opportunism, local and sectional loyalty and, above all, a strong belief that the individual is responsible to the family rather than to the state.

These attitudes make effective government difficult, though General Park and his colleagues are endeavoring to bring about changes. The Korean political mind unfortunately does not seem to have acknowledged that civil servants can be

167

incorruptible, that lawmakers can deliberate on the basis of national rather than personal interest, and that elected officials need not pay off election debts to a favored few. Internal turmoil exists and will undoubtedly continue as the Republic of Korea seeks to achieve its goal of a free and democratic government.

The major problem facing the ROK is defense against Communist aggression. Over 500,000 soldiers are kept in training and in position to repel attacks. Though they grow some agricultural produce for their own consumption, these soldiers are a heavy drain on the economy. Large American military aid funds are devoted to equipment and material for the Korean armed forces. This military burden will continue to be of major importance to the Park government.

The North Korean regime is constantly seeking to subvert the ROK. Communist agents are sent into South Korea to stir up anti-government agitation and to corrupt, if possible, South Korean political figures. Broadcasts are made from North Korea to project an image of a stable government, earnest in its desire for the "peaceful unification of the homeland." Offers are made to expedite visits to reunify families and for trade across the Truce Line. "Imperialistic" United States is berated as blocking these peaceful efforts. The ROK, in part, because of its instability throughout its existence, must be vigilant in counteracting these propaganda moves. Perhaps the most potent defensive weapons the ROK could bring forth would be effective programs of economic and social development to better the lot of all of the people of South Korea.

XII. *Economic Development of South Korea*

The people and government of South Korea face serious economic problems. The growth in population, increasing at a rate of 2.9 percent a year, is not being matched by stepped-up economic production. Standards of living are unchanged or falling. The number of unemployed, particularly in the cities, is relatively large. In the rural areas there is much under-employment. High on the list of causes for these economic ills is the relatively inadequate resource base of South Korea. Mineral and hydroelectric resources are few. The agricultural land has been used for centuries. Only small amounts of new land have been reclaimed; existing fields are being worked intensively, with increasing amounts of commercial fertilizers. Though crop production has increased greatly in recent decades, still, farms are small, averaging 2.2 acres in size, and inefficient. Hand labor is employed intensively. The marketing structure for agricultural products creaks under fluctuating governmental price policies.

South Korea is not an industrialized country although some factories have been built, often with outside capital in the form of government grants. The nation still depends upon the import of many products and has a large trade deficit. A trained labor force is needed and there is a particularly great shortage in management at the middle and higher levels.

The tertiary industries—commerce, transportation services to the public, health, education—have been more successful but still face barriers to expansion. A major obstacle is the cycle of inflation which has retarded sound movement. Unfortunately, petty graft and corrupt practices have increased instability in the economy.

Despite these problems the economic picture is not completely black. The very fact that there has been no collapse is encouraging. One vital factor has been the infusion of grants, loans, and technical assistance, particularly from the United States. Joint Korean-American committees have worked together to develop plans for the economy as a whole and for its various sectors. These plans have had to take into account the military situation, for defense expenditures and the drain in manpower for military service have been heavy. There is a strong desire to maintain a healthy private sector in the economy rather than to have a socialized, highly managed economy. The complexities of the economic development of Korea are beginning to be recognized by Korean leaders, who realize that their survival in power depends upon their skill in meeting the needs of the Korean people.

Agricultural Development

Almost two-thirds of the people of South Korea gain their livelihood from agriculture. The major crop continues to be rice. It occupies more than a third of the acreage and furnishes three-fourths of the value of grain production. For improvements to be made in the agricultural sector of the economy, rice production must be increased. A plentiful and well-controlled water supply of the paddy fields is of paramount importance for increasing yields. At present, most of the fields are dependent upon rain falling on them or in the immediate vicinity. Relatively few large-scale irrigation projects exist, but farm land supplied from these projects is much less dependent upon the vagaries of nature and can produce good crops year after year. Other measures have been adopted to increase production: better selection of seeds, more careful transplanting, increased use of commercial fertilizer, and better harvesting practices. Even so, much of the yield depends upon the weather during critical parts of the growing and harvesting season. As a consequence, rice production varies from bumper crop to poor crop, with dire results for the farmer.

With the defeat and departure of the Japanese and the end of their exploitive agricultural policies, a major land reform was imperative. Because of the uncertain political situation no one was in a position to make broad-reaching decisions. Finally, however, the American authorities (the largest landlords in Korea) disposed of the land formerly owned by the Japanese and which they then held by distributing it to the tenants. Repayments were to be made over a period of years. The distribution of land owned by Korean landlords (many of whom had been collaborators with the Japanese) was delayed by the Korean War but eventually did take place. Unfortunately, the economic benefits of land reform were negated to some extent by the high rate of monetary inflation and by the fluctuation of government investment policies. In subsequent years, Korean landlords have begun to reappear, amalgamating small, inefficient holdings; however, these larger holdings are still fairly small as compared to those of the pre-World War II period.

The commercialization of agriculture in South Korea has been spurred by rapidly growing cities and the extensive military and government establishment. The government sets the

171

MAJOR CROPS IN THE
REPUBLIC OF KOREA, 1962*

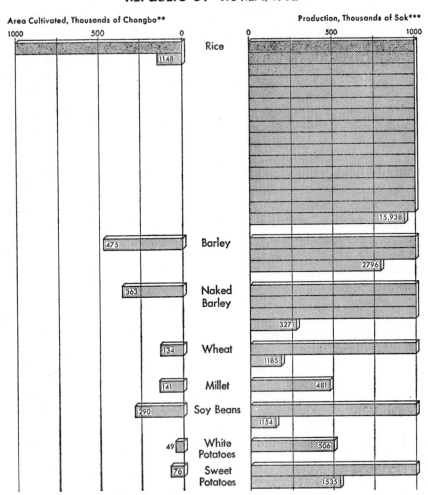

Area Cultivated, Thousands of Chongbo**

1000   500   0

Production, Thousands of Sok***

0   500   1000

Crop	Area	Production
Rice	1148	15,938
Barley	475	2796
Naked Barley	363	327
Wheat	134	1185
Millet	141	481
Soy Beans	290	1154
White Potatoes	49	506
Sweet Potatoes	76	1535

*Minor crops totaled 310,000 chongbo

**One thousand chongbo equals 2450 acres

***One thousand sok equals 4960 bushels

172

prices and is a major buyer of rice (in part through tax in kind) and a major seller of fertilizer, but its policies are unrealistic and lack continuity; so the desired stability of agriculture has still not been achieved in South Korea.

In 1962, considered an average year, South Korea produced the amounts of agricultural crops shown on the accompanying chart. It is obvious from this chart that rice with a production of 16,000,000 *sok* (one sok equals 4.96 bushels) is the primary crop. Yet it also shows the significant production of barley, naked barley, wheat, millet, soybeans, and potatoes. Barley, which totals 6,000,000 sok, is grown as a winter crop, often double cropped with rice or with dry crops such as beans and cotton. Meaningful production figures for vegetable crops are difficult to obtain, for most of these are grown in small plots near the farmers' homes. They are not sold commercially in the same way that the basic grains are sold but have an important place in the agricultural economy nevertheless.

The livestock industry of Korea has been developing rapidly and holds some real promise for the future. Cattle are used largely as beasts of burden: to pull carts, plow fields, and move grinding wheels. Only a few are used for beef and hides. Dairy cattle are kept mainly near the large cities, where there is a market for fresh milk and milk products. Pigs are common in many farmyards, feeding on the farmyard waste and foraging in the fields after the harvest. Sheep and goats are not so common, though efforts have been made to foster their introduction, particularly in the upland areas. Every farmyard has its chickens. Eggs are a common food to be bought in village markets. In olden days they were nestled in rice straw strings of ten eggs each; now they are put in paper sacks or boxes.

The Korean farmer depends on the forested hills around his village for wood and brush for his home fires. Many of the hill slopes were used by the villages communally. Under

173

the increased commercialization and government control of the Japanese, these forested lands, which the villagers for centuries had considered theirs to do with as they wished, were subject to regulation. At the time of Korea's liberation, controls over excessive cutting were neglected and great harm was done by the destitute and desperate farmers. However, more recently, extensive reforestation programs have been instituted. Countless seedlings dot the hills with green. To a visitor to Korea after an absence of some years this is a dramatic and promising sight. In the long run, these forests will be a great economic asset to Korea, not only for the timber and firewood they can produce but for needed protection from erosion and damage to the agricultural lands in the valleys.

The waters around the Korean peninsula contain many good fishing grounds. These were exploited by the Japanese, often by fishing fleets based in Japanese ports. Disputes over fishing rights arose with the formation of the Republic of Korea. In 1955, Syngman Rhee reinforced Korean claims to the area within the so-called Rhee Line by seizing Japanese fishing boats which were on the Korean side. The Rhee Line actually was a demarcation made by General MacArthur after the surrender of the Japanese a decade before; it defined areas of jurisdiction of the occupying authorities. It was reinforced during the Korean War for military reasons. The Rhee Line, following geodetic lines, extends in places as far as sixty miles off the coast of Korea. Its continuation had been a source of constant friction between the Japanese and the Koreans.

After independence, the Korean fishing industry was slow in recovering for it lacked the managerial skills of the Japanese. However, by 1960, fisheries production totaled 357,182 tons. Most of this (241,737 tons) was fish, but there was also a significant collection of shellfish and seaweed. A five-year plan for fisheries development projected an annual fish haul by 1966 of 590,000 tons. It would require new equipment in boats and nets, that ports be developed with refrigeration plants, fishermen trained, and deep-sea fishing fleets sent to other Asian waters. Much of this recovery would be assisted by American aid.

Industrial Development

The Republic of Korea, in separation from North Korea, lacks mineral and hydroelectric power resources. During the days of Japanese control when Korea was unified, a flow of raw materials, particularly of coal and electric power, poured down from north to south Korea. The electric power supply was continued until May, 1948, when North Korea exerted political pressure by cutting it off. The Koreans in the south, with the assistance of the United States and other nations, have subsequently been engaged in numerous projects to develop the resource base.

The major coal resources are the deposits of anthracite coal in the Yongwol area in southeastern Korea. A railroad line has been built through rugged terrain to tap this area. A thermal electric power plant, cement plants and some chemical industries now utilize this resource. Tungsten deposits exist in scattered localities in Korea, also gold and silver deposits. Copper, lead, zinc, and manganese production is minor. South Korea is not a rich area for mineral production.

The Park government in its recent planning has emphasized the need to expand electric power production as one of three "strategic sectors," along with agriculture and public works. It is obvious that without this energy, modern industrialization is not possible. The present supply of electric power is estimated to be less than three-fourths of the basic requirements. There are thermal electric power plants in the major cities of Seoul and Pusan and smaller plants, often powered by imported petroleum, in the smaller cities. On the upper

Han River a hydroelectric power plant was rehabilitated after the Korean War. Other small hydroelectric plants have been established on a dual purpose basis, their major function being flood control and irrigation. But large-scale capital outlays are needed if great amounts of power are to be produced economically.

Shortage of capital has also affected manufacturing industries in South Korea. Most are small and devoted to production of consumer goods. Any large-scale industries have been built largely with aid from the United States. As a consequence many of them are state-owned or state-controlled and they suffer from inefficiencies and lack of managerial skills. Often, for political reasons and as a form of government subsidy, prices of their products are set too low for economic operation. After years of delays a large-scale fertilizer plant was finally opened at Chungju in 1962, and also an iron works at Pusan. A plate glass factory started with United Nations assistance has recently been enlarged. Cement plants, chemical industries, shipbuilding and repair yards are examples of large scale industries that are being developed, though haltingly.

Over three-quarters of the value of manufactured output comes from industries such as textiles, rubber shoes, paper, bicycles, cigarettes, beer, food processing and other consumer goods. Though these operate mainly in the private sector of the economy, they are subject to varying control through price fixing, interest rates, and taxing policies of the government. Most of these industries are located in the suburbs of the major cities, close to the markets. In addition, cottage industries making traditional Korean handicraft—pottery, lacquer-ware, silk, cotton, and hemp textiles—have survived in home workshops in the towns and villages of South Korea.

Because of market demands, industry in South Korea is

176

likely to continue to grow. However, there are numerous prerequisites—for one, firm government policies fostering such growth. Vocational training of the plentiful supply of unskilled labor is another need. As trade with Japan develops, adequate safeguards must be set up. Much of the Koreans' antipathy for the Japanese is due to a fear that if normal economic relations with Japan were to be recreated, the fledgling Korean industries would decline, for they could not compete with imported Japanese-made consumer products. Yet with proper protection of Korean rights, imported Japanese capital and technical skills could be beneficial to industrial development.

Commercial Development

After the liberation of Korea Japanese influence on the country's commercial life was completely halted. The Japanese were repatriated and Koreans assumed power. This meant that Korean clerks with very little previous training and experience were suddenly becoming store managers. Family connections, always of importance in the Korean-owned private concerns, were permitted to influence those commercial concerns that had been Japanese owned and were now being run by the government. Graft and corruption compounded the problem until the business life of Korea sadly deteriorated. Integrity was especially needed in banking but, unhappily, was lacking here too. Differing exchange rates gave special advantages to charitable groups and to business engaged in foreign trade activities. Unfortunately, a black market of considerable magnitude in foreign currency and U. S. military notes flourished. The fluctuating government policies on prices added to the general chaos.

Despite the difficulties, commerce has revived. The seasonal markets in the villages, towns, and cities continue to be of

major importance in the commercial life of the individual Korean family. Shops and stores have sprung up, although sometimes their stocks of merchandise are limited. Gradually a mercantile class has come into being to take the place of the Japanese merchants. These are healthy developments and show some promise for the future.

The Koreans have become much more mobile. Buses, jitneys, and trucks, often kept together only by rare ingenuity, provide transport in the rural areas. Many new roads have been constructed, some for military purposes. Since the Korean War road transport has increased through the use of old military equipment. The railroads, damaged during the war, have been rebuilt and some new lines opened up. A Korean air line provides service to the major cities. The ports have been improved to care for military imports.

Foreign trade continues to be in a deficit position, particularly with the drop of trade with Japan. Much imported grain and supplies are sold in commercial channels and provide counterpart funds for military and other expenditures. However, the international trade situation improved more decidedly after the military coup and the installation of the Park government. Efforts have been made to restore trade with Japan. (Actually, quite a bit of illicit trade had been carried on directly with Japan or through Hong Kong.) Japanese investors are showing some interest in Korean business and industry despite the hesitancy of the Koreans and their fear of Japanese economic power. Korean exports which had been around $40,000,000 grew rapidly to reach a peak of $120,000,000 in 1964, and are projected to reach $200,000,000 in 1966. Though there has been some optimistic talk of the reaching of a "take off" point in the economy, it is obvious that long-term credits and grants from abroad are still needed if the Korean economy is to keep up its recent rate of growth.

Urban Developments

The Koreans have always had their roots in the countryside but these ties have been increasingly broken and a new type of urban society has evolved. The extended family has become of less importance. People are being crowded together and treated impersonally. Schools take young people away from the homes. Christian churches have developed new centers for the society, cutting across traditional social lines. Mass entertainment, such as movies and sports events, are city phenomena. There is more rush and clatter; the speed of movement in the cities is always a shock to the visitor from the countryside.

During the Korean War many of the cities were severely damaged. Much of the population had fled to the countryside, a few had gotten within the Pusan perimeter or to Cheju Island. The wholesale reshuffling of people that took place during the Korean War increased the trend toward urbanization after the war. Seoul and its suburbs have a population of over 3,000,000 today. Pusan, Taegu, and many other cities have had equivalent percentages of growth. Thus, South Korea is becoming more and more an urbanized society. This has been so rapid that slums and large tracts of simple uniform houses are now common characteristics of the cities of Korea. Transit systems, sewage disposal works, water supply facilities and all the other needs for large cities are all greatly overtaxed by this rapid growth. Though there have been some efforts to preserve space for parks, to widen major streets and to take other actions to alleviate the inevitable squalor of certain sections of the cities, urban planning is still not too far advanced.

The economic future of South Korea is not bright. The relatively limited natural resources, the devastation created by the Korean War and the threat of its renewal, the large amount of the gross national product which must be devoted

179

to military defense, the lack of broadly based vocational and technical training programs, the rapid urbanization without adequate planning are major hindrances. Correct balances between agriculture, industry, and commerce, between rural and urban life, must be developed. Certainly the emphasis on the "strategic sectors," increased agricultural production, expansion of electric power production, and improvement of transportation and other facilities through public works, is soundly conceived. But to achieve a sound economy a large influx of private and governmental capital and aid, both in goods and technical assistance is a prime necessity. President Park in a speech in New York on May 20, 1965, optimistically stated: "To put it frankly, the Korean economy has reached just a step away from that which they call the take-off point. Therefore, inviting foreign capital and technical assistance into the country is the most pressing need of its economy at the present stage."

XIII. *Cultural Development of South Korea*

Changes in the social and cultural life of South Korea have been particularly marked since the Korean War. Decades of Japanese control and the turmoil since 1945 have scarcely been conducive to cultural growth, but now the people of South Korea are free and they face very real problems in acquiring a sense of responsibility to match their new freedom. Their great attachment to the past and desire to retain a distinctly Korean culture gives them a strong base on which to build. Yet the pressure of the outside world, the severe economic poverty, and the constant threat of war do not encourage the flowering of cultural activities so devoutly wished. There is ferment in all cultural fields which gives promise of action but a lack of any real unifying force.

Many Koreans tend to follow fads rather than develop their own methods of expression. The numerous universities and the multitude of learned societies are grouped about certain strong personalities and their adherents. There is not sufficient crossing of lines in cultural fields or sufficient communication of ideas. It is easy to condemn this weakness, but to the South Korean people it is by far preferable to the regimentation which curtails individual expression among their fellow-countrymen in North Korea.

Educational Development

In the revitalization of Korean cultural life the vast expansion of the educational system has been of particular importance. It is almost as though learning, always revered, is now looked upon as a panacea for all the ills of the land. Teachers and students have power and hold an important place in the social and political life of South Korea today. Students gave impetus to the forces leading to the downfall of the Syngman Rhee regime. Today, student-led protests against normalization of Korean-Japanese relations, against corruption in government, and in favor of an expanded economy are common occurrences. Too frequent use of student pressure groups for inconsequential problems or situations has inevitably weakened the traditionally respected position of students, however.

Basic literacy in Korea has increased greatly. One of the benefits of the Korean phonetic writing system, *hangul* (literally "national language" and now reduced to twenty-four symbols), has been that it could be quickly learned by those who speak Korean. Soon after independence widespread literacy campaigns were instituted. Though in 1945, 78 percent of the population over the age of twelve was illiterate, by 1952 only 25 percent was illiterate, and the percentage is much lower today. New textbooks and reading materials are prepared in hangul. Newspapers and magazines still mix Chinese characters with the phonetic symbols, but there has been a concerted move to limit the number of complex characters used. With the increase of literacy, the Korean people have become better informed. Some creative writers use hangul for novels, short stories and poems. Technical materials, particularly related to improvement of agriculture, have also been published in this simple-to-read system.

Though adult literacy programs continue to be of importance, the major effort is devoted to the development of a large-scale formal educational program. Prior to 1945 educators slavishly imitated the military-inspired Japanese system. With the liberation of Korea, new textbooks, new curricula, and new organizations have been instituted. The aim is universal compulsory education for the first six years of schooling, to be followed by voluntary education at the upper levels. Unfortunately, the financial resources available have not been sufficient to achieve the aims for universal education. One development has been the widespread organization of parents' associations, literally called "PTA" in Korean. Member parents are usually required to donate funds for providing equipment and supplementing teachers' salaries, or to give time to help build facilities. In 1962 the government abolished the PTA organization for political reasons, though "School Supporters Associations" continue to collect fees and make donations. Tuition is paid for both public and private schools and parents must buy books and supplies for their children.

Despite improvements, a shortage of facilities, of funds, and of teachers still exists, holding back many of those who crave educational opportunities. Certain weaknesses continue, some of them inherited from the past. Schools are operated very authoritatively; discipline is harsh. Much learning is by rote and tremendous emphasis is put upon passing examinations for entrance to school and for graduation. Not enough emphasis is put upon technical and vocational education, although the economy calls for it. The tradition of the scholar—aloof from all contact with manual work and reading his literary classics, following the lines of characters with his long fingernail—is still too strong.

Roughly, 90 percent of the children attend elementary schools. There were in 1962, 4,089,152 elementary school pupils. Three out of four of the teachers and almost all of the principals are men. The secondary schools are divided into two levels: middle and high school, each three years in length. After elementary school the boys and girls have to pass rigorous examinations for admission to middle school. There they are generally separated and study slightly different curricula, particularly in vocational subjects. Out of the total enrollment of 655,123 students in middle schools in 1962, 267,270 were in privately supported schools, though some financial support is given to these schools by the local government. At the high school level the 338 academic high schools with 199,253 students were evenly divided between public and private support. The Park government's aim is to hold the number of academic high schools at the present level and devote effort to developing 800 vocational and technical high schools, though in 1962 only 125,341 full- and part-time students were enrolled in such schools.

An interesting feature of the Korean higher educational pattern is the existence of many privately supported colleges. Some of these had their origin decades ago through missionary efforts. One of the most famous colleges is Methodist-supported Ewha. It numbers among the largest women's universities in the world; in 1962 it had 7,351 students. It has had great influence in educating women leaders in Korea. Other missionary-related colleges are Yonsei, formed by amalgamating the Chosen Christian College for men and the Severance Medical College, with a student population of 5,425 in 1962, and Soongsil, which traces its origin to the former Union Christian College (of which the author's father was President), located in North Korea in Pyongyang. Many other private and church-related colleges and universities have been established with funds raised abroad or donated by

184

wealthy Koreans. Altogether in 1962 there were thirty-six private colleges and twenty-four private junior colleges. Not all of these institutions have high standards; some might even be called diploma mills. In 1962 the government drastically curtailed the number of private colleges and the students they could admit.

The state-supported system of higher education includes a group of regional colleges and universities, located mostly in the provincial capitals. In 1962 there were twenty-five of these institutions. The public educational pyramid culminates in Seoul National University, which occupies in part the former campus of the Keijo Imperial University of Japanese days. It was students from this university, as well as from other colleges and high schools, who led the student revolt in the spring of 1960. (An interesting footnote is that the first outburst actually took place at a ceremony welcoming new students to the university.) The total higher education enrollment throughout Korea in 1962 was 103,816 men and 24,741 women. From 1952 to 1962, 212 doctoral degrees were granted.

Drama and Music

The Korean people put great faith in the educational process not only as a key to the future economic and social development of their nation but also as a curator of their cultural heritage. This is a rich heritage and is evidenced in literature, art, and music. Though, as has been previously pointed out, much of the formal culture has been derived from the Chinese traditions, the Koreans have put their own distinctive stamp on their classical works of art and literature. In modern times Korean artists and writers have increasingly been using local themes and writing in the vernacular. Once freed from Japanese regressive controls, new artists and writers came forth with new works in a rapid outpouring. Some of these have not stood the test of even so short

185

a time, but a few will survive. The Korean War, ideological conflicts, and the varying viewpoints of different generations are common themes in Korean art, music, and literature today.

Modern media of artistic expression; the motion picture, the formal stage, the ballet, and the symphony orchestra are enjoyed by Koreans. Though much is copied from the West, the themes used in these media are often Korean in character. Old classics, such as the "Fragrance of Spring," and adaptations from Korean folklore are used in dances, plays, and music. Interesting attempts are being made to exploit these new media in avant-garde ways, not always with sure-fire success. In art as in other facets of Korean life, conflicting and shifting schools of expression are found, often grouped about a single artistic personality.

The motion picture has enjoyed a tremendous modern vogue in Korea. There were studios in Korea in the 1920's and 30's that produced some 200 films. Notable among them were "Arirang" and "Ferryboat," which had nationalistic themes. Some motion pictures were made in Japan with Korean subjects and actors. The bulk of the films shown, however, were Japanese or Western imports. It has been in the post-liberation period and particularly after the Korean War that motion pictures have flourished in Korea. Two of the major handicaps to the industry have been lack of firm financial support and absence of modern technical equipment. Tax benefits have aided greatly. One reason for the popularity of films in Korea has been their use for education and entertainment in the military services. Documentaries are greatly enhancing adult education and information programs. Sixteen-millimeter film also saves on costs of production and showing for some commercial motion pictures.

Motion pictures lend themselves to the Korean love of fantasy. The film "Fragrance of Spring" in 35 millimeter color was a tremendous commercial success in 1955. It was fol-

186

lowed by many other films based on old Korean stories, for good modern scripts were not readily available. Many pictures are made on meager budgets and in great haste, but the Koreans enjoy their own films greatly and react with enthusiasm to them. They are not averse to showing their emotions. A movie theatre is apt to be a noisy place with loud audience participation in laughter and audible weeping.

The stage and the ballet have not met with so much success. In Seoul many of the plays are Korean translations or adaptations of Western drama, some are old classics modernized. The formal ballet follows the same pattern. No genuine Korean style of drama and dance have evolved.

Folk dances and plays, which were not encouraged under the Japanese, are being revived with widespread participation in many of the rural areas of Korea. In some of these plays, for example in villages along the southeast coast, old stylized masks are used even today. The village dances and plays are usually performed on the nights of full moon, particularly at the New Year and after the rice harvest. Farmers' bands and dancers move from village to village to put on their entertainments. These are spontaneous efforts on the part of the people to keep alive old local traditions. They reflect the joy and pride in their regained nationalism. Through the schools in particular, some of the local dances have been modernized and standardized, often losing something in the process. It is common, however, to see large numbers of students and young people putting on these stylized versions at field days or on national holidays to the accompaniment of a scratchy record or tape recorder blaring out over a loud speaker.

Much more sophisticated than the folk dances and songs were the dances and songs of the kisangs, or dancing girls. A talented kisang was able to converse intelligently on a wide range of subjects, to write or recite poetry, and to draw

187

from a fund of stories and sayings for the amusement of her listeners. Under the Japanese kisangs became more like the lower class of Japanese geisha. Just as has happened with the geisha in modern days, the old tradition of the cultured, highly trained and respected kisang is passing from the scene. Recent reforms on the part of the present regime are spelling her doom. Now the record player or the tape recorder, manipulated by a bar girl, furnishes the entertainment for the popular restaurant or coffee shop. It blasts out stylized Korean folk music played on Western instruments, or Western music ranging from a choice of classic symphonies to jazz.

With the opening of Korea to the outside world Western-style music became popular, due in part to the decadence and stereotyping into which Korean music had fallen in the later decades of the Yi dynasty. The early Protestant missionaries introduced hymns with Korean translations or words set to traditional tunes and taught Western music in the schools they established. The Japanese had also adopted Western music and instruments and through the school curricula these were fostered in Korea. The Koreans made the adaptation quite readily. A number of musicians became well trained in these new media, some went to Europe and the United States for further training. With the liberation of Korea and the large numbers of Westerners in Korea, modern forms of music, ranging from "rock-'n-roll" to symphonies, were increasingly in demand. Yet this was accompanied by the revival of old Korean forms of music, motivated largely by nationalistic feelings.

Art

Amidst the very volatile Korean society the creative artist has no easy existence. Economic pressures are not conducive to financial security. As is so often the lot of the artist everywhere, many a would-be artist in Korea must spend his energy and time painting garish billboards to gain a livelihood. The streets of the cities are a weird jumble of these signs and placards; there is little beauty in popular art. But all the while, in colleges and universities and in the quiet of homes and workshops, aspiring artists are trying to revive a vital Korean artistic tradition.

Some Korean musicians, artists and writers, unsympathetic to political events and attracted by better financial returns, have left Korea for the United States and Europe. A few have met with considerable success. It would be regrettable if their genius were to be lost permanently to Korea. Creative talents in Korean artistic fields need all the nourishment and support they can get in these days of increasingly materialistic and nonhumanistic pressures.

Formerly Korean artists had the traditions of the past to inspire them, but during the days of Japanese control there was little impetus and few opportunities for creative painters, potters, and architects. Artists and craftsmen, particularly those who studied in Japan, imitated the Japanese or copied old masters, rather than permitting the development of modern Korean schools. They embarked on all sorts of projects and tried all manners of expression, only to be frustrated again by the devastating Korean War. For architects this war may have been a blessing in disguise, for in the years since 1945 they had been trying to break away from the old styles of Western architecture; now they are following the latest trends being developed in the United States and Europe.

Other forms of art, calligraphy, sculpture, pottery, and brass work have continued, but in comparison with the old Korean classic works they seem to lack artistic merit. The statues of modern political figures in North and in South Korea are hardly artistic sculpture. Memorial pylons have been erected that are often travesties of the heritage of Korean sculpture, being neither modern nor traditional. There has been some increase in folk art, such as lacquer work with mother-of-pearl inlays, but these pieces with their rather garish effects cater more to a commercial market.

Modern Korean painters may be grouped in two distinctive schools. One group follows the traditional Oriental painting of scrolls and small paintings. Their medium is brush and ink on paper, a technique which they learn usually as apprentices of older artists. Some of them follow the old Korean styles closely, with natural subjects, such as mountains and streams, flowers and birds. Others are experimenting with Western perspectives and realism and still others are trying to develop entirely new artistic expressions while still using the old media. The other school follows Occidental painting. Some Koreans who had gone to Japan to study returned with knowledge of new techniques of oil and water-color painting. Some of their works were shown in the annual exhibit sponsored by the Japanese Government-General. They used Western techniques and no forms that were uniquely Korean seemed to emerge. In the free atmosphere that followed liberation, Korean artists adopted numerous new trends from the West; one of the popular schools was a neorealist group. A major split divided the painters, as it did the writers, between leftists who used art for political purposes and those who believed that they should practice art for art's sake. Here too, were numerous cliques and factions, often grouped about a single painter and his disciples. An active group of modernists does exist whose paintings are largely influenced by the modern art of the West. Some of their works show real promise, particularly when Korean themes are used.

Literature

The Korean people have continued to appreciate literature and count on it to help preserve their cultural heritage. During the days of Japanese control there were some writers who helped to enrich the heritage and to keep the national language and national feeling alive. Their writings are still read in South Korea. Much of the literature marked a break with the past by using less classical forms or new forms of literary expression, many of them based upon Western examples. Peter H. Lee in his book, *Korean Literature: Topics and Themes,* 1964, stresses the deleterious influence of the Japanese over Korean literary development in these words:

"During the period of thirty-six years from the annexation to the end of the Second World War, the new literature was forced to grow in the shadow of Japanese colonialism. It was doomed to be the literature of an exploited people. Denied the spirit of freedom and dynamism, the new literature in Korea became one of sorrow, reflecting a grief-stricken and despondent outlook. Without the indomitable spirit of the Korean people, Korean literature by itself could neither have preserved the Korean language, which embodies and manifests Korean tradition and culture, nor revealed the ultimate quality of the Korean sensibility. It was a triumph of the Korean spirit that it preserved and continued the Korean language despite Japanese oppression."

One of the most interesting writers of this period was Choe Namson who is well-known for his lyrical phrasing of the Korean Declaration of Independence written at the time of the Mansei movement in 1919. Mainly a novelist and essayist, he was also a poet who wrote some inspiring verses for children. Another writer of this period, Yi Kwangsu, wrote modern historical and social novels with strong nationalistic overtones. The modern novelists used the Korean language and Korean scenes and characters. Students who returned from Japan wrote poems and novels that were influenced in form by current Japanese writing. A leftist group of writers emerged in the mid 1920's opposing the romanticism of Korean literature. However, it was suppressed by the Japanese in 1935.

191

Certain writers sought to escape from censorship and reality with fantasies and "pure" poetry.

After liberation, there was a tremendous outflow of literary publications, some of it Communist-inspired. Considerable conflict arose in literary circles. Some writers refused to succumb to modern trends and continued to write on traditional Korean themes, emphasizing love of nature. Others were influenced by Western poetic and literary forms and gave attention to style rather than content. A group of writers who had been directly involved in the Korean War as young soldiers began writing of the war, sometimes through symbolism, or, in contrast, a purposeful escape from the realities of war. Writers were intensely aware of literary developments throughout the world and fervently desired Korea to be a part of these developments.

Mass Media

In order for literature to flourish, publication outlets must exist. Many Korean poems, short stories, and novels were printed in "little magazines" which sprang up only to wither and die after a few issues. Some were sponsored by colleges or societies, others by political groups. Under the Japanese there had been constant problems of censorship and of lack of financial support. Naturally trashy stories, risqué or highly romantic, had good sales, disheartening the serious writers, as so often happens throughout the world. Korean publishers were few in number and rarely lasted. The Japanese exerted increasingly rigorous control, but in 1945 freedom brought a great boom in publishing. Demand for text books and for reading material of all kinds was tremendous. Paper and printing equipment were in short supply, however, though some were imported under foreign aid programs. Magazines flourished, principally the light entertainment variety, including the inevitable movie and adventure magazines. Serious journals, such as *Sasangge* (Thought), had limited circulation.

Though gossip sessions in the village and exchange of information at the markets in town are still major means of communication, new methods—the radio, the newspaper, the government bulletin, and the magazine—have acquired importance, particularly in the towns and cities. Many of the common media are under government ownership and are used to propagate and inform the public of government programs and policies. They are improving their methods of presentation, yet they still remain suspect to the people. Since the days of the Japanese the average Korean has had little confidence in this type of pronouncement.

Private newspapers have been one of the free media, though with a freedom subject to varying political conditions. Under the Japanese, the Korean newspapers were under strict control. These newspapers were key instruments in keeping alive the use of hangul, the national alphabet, as well as other Korean nationalistic manifestations. When the Japanese relaxed their strict controls in the 1920's as an aftermath of the Mansei movement of 1919, three daily newspapers under Korean ownership were permitted: the *Dong-a,* the *Choson,* and the *Choson Chunang* newspapers. However, they still remained under heavy censorship and were frequently suppressed for varying periods of time. The *Dong-a* newspaper was confiscated 489 times during a twenty-year period, for example. As World War II approached the newspapers were forced to stop publication.

Two of the prewar papers, the *Dong-a* and the *Choson,* started up again after liberation. Others also began publishing, sometimes sponsored by a particular political group. One had support from a group of Catholic laymen; others were designed for the North Koreans in refuge in Seoul. Following the traditions of Korean newspapers of Japanese days,

193

the newspapers were, as a matter of principle, "anti-government." The Rhee regime continued government censorship and interference—with damaging results, for newspapers were an important factor in the overthrow of Rhee.

Complete freedom of the press was granted by the Chang government but the newspapers did not operate responsibly under their new freedom. Often the chief purpose of the new journals and papers that appeared was blackmail—extracting funds and favors from persons whom they threatened with exposure of past sins. Thus, instead of attacking corruption, a major weakness, some newspapers added corrupt practices of their own. Such irresponsibility was partly responsible for the widespread support given by the public to the military coup. Freedom of the press was rescinded and the newspapers once again were under strict government censorship and control. Some of them have been suspended or closed; most of the so-called newspapers of the Chang period have disappeared. Though there has been some loosening of control, many of the newspapers of today echo official policies and are not allowed to contribute so much as they should to the development of a thinking democratic society.

The Koreans had possessed some radios during Japanese days, but after the war transistorized and cheap receivers became readily available, and made radio an important medium of mass communication. This fact was well recognized by the United States military authorities, who took over the control of many small stations in Seoul and other cities. News and cultural programs were broadcast and radio also contributed toward Korean language development. The ROK assumed control in 1948, and most of the stations in Seoul, destroyed during the Korean War, were subsequently rebuilt with increased power and range. Programs included children's hours, quiz shows, amateur contests, Western and Korean music, serials and plays, and lectures. These were heavily

194

interspersed with news, sometimes slanted, and government releases. In 1955 a private station was licensed; it was a Christian station which included a great amount of worthwhile music. The U. S. military maintained radio stations for their troops and a TV network with American programming. Koreans who understood English listened to these stations. (A Korean TV station in Seoul was sponsored by an American company in order to sell TV sets, but it was not very successful and after a severe fire it went off the air.) Both the U. S. military stations (whose Korean language programs originate largely from Okinawa) and ROK stations are beamed to North Korea for political purposes. North Korean stations in response sound away on their basic themes: the evils of the American "imperialists" and benefits of living under their own North Korean regime.

Religion

Economic pressures, social change, and rapid modernization have profoundly affected the mores of South Koreans and have sent many on a quest for religious beliefs in which they may find strength, solace, and stability. All men look for meaning in their lives, but the Koreans have a despairing urgency in their search. The old gods have not fulfilled their needs; new gods must be found.

The old religious base of Korea—the folkways, the beliefs in supernatural spirits, the practices of the sorcerers, the almost universal feeling for a supreme being—continues to be significant, however. This unorganized religious heritage remains in the background, and sometimes parts of it have been used to lend support to new religious practices. In South Korea, as contrasted to the North, there has been relative freedom for the people to search out new religious ideas. No official state religion exists, though individual leaders have been known for their own religious connections: Syngman

Rhee, a Methodist; John M. Chang, a Catholic; and General Park, with Buddhist background.

One common characteristic among all the organized religions in South Korea in recent years has been the virulence of internal schisms and conflicts. Buddhist priests who practice celibacy strive to exclude from their privileges priests who are married. Confucian scholars argue with vehemence certain differences in the classics and the historical Korean interpretation of them. Chundogyo, the native Korean religion, has suffered a split in leadership and emphasis. Catholics are divided into different mission groups, for example, the French and the American mission fathers carry on differing programs to improve the economic conditions of their parishioners. Protestant churches have divided and subdivided and many new Pentecostal groups have started up.

Sports

In modern Korea, many of the traditional sports have been forgotten. The rock fights were the first to be forbidden. New, more sophisticated Western sports began to be introduced through the schools. Baseball and tennis could not be played very widely because of the costly equipment and facilities necessary. Soccer, basketball, and volleyball were very popular, however. Skating in winter and swimming in summer were favorite sports. The Koreans were particularly adept in track and field competition. A high point was reached when a Korean won the marathon at the 1936 Olympics. (A Korean newspaper touched up his photograph so that the Japanese rising sun symbol on his shirt disappeared; as a result, the newspaper was suspended for six months!)

Koreans engage particularly in sports which can be carried on individually without equipment. It is common to see young men jogging along the streets at night or early in the morning, training to be long distance runners. Track received a big boost when a Korean won the Boston Marathon. In the military camps physical fitness through sports is encouraged. Interestingly, it was over the subject of a joint team, required by Olympic rules in 1964, that the North and South Korean representatives met on neutral grounds. The desire for a team was great and they came close to reaching an agreement, but finally even athletics fell victim to political cleavage.

Certainly, in all of its varied phases the cultural scene of South Korea today is changing. It is hoped that in the course of these changes a sound Korean culture will emerge—one that will be neither a slavish imitation of the West nor a pale copy of the Korean past. Given the grave economic, social, and political difficulties South Korea faces today, as well as the ever-present threat of war, it is surprising that art and culture have made any progress at all—but they have. This perseverance is characteristic of the Koreans—to search, despite vicissitudes, for beauty and meaning in life, and to give expression to these through whatever channels are open to them.

XIV.   Korea in the Modern World

Korea cannot be separated from the rest of the world. The Koreans learned this hard fact when the doors of their hermit nation were forced open in 1876. Korea was brought vividly into international politics when the United Nations went into action in the Korean War in 1950. The future of Korea depends more on the behavior of governments in Moscow, Washington, New York, and Peking than of those in Pyongyang and Seoul—a reality that is hard for Koreans, both north and south of the Truce Line, to accept.

The division of Korea by the 38th parallel was the result of quickly made military decisions. The aftermath has been two Koreas, divided by a Truce Line, both of them unwilling pawns in the global struggle between the Communist world and the Free World. Not only politically but economically, the Korean people are dependent upon other nations. A unified, free, and democratic Korea is far from accomplishment.

There seems to be little progress toward a peaceful settlement of the problems occasioned by the division of Korea.

198

The hope was expressed at the conclusion of the Geneva Conferences in 1954, that "after a time, when the inevitable passions stirred up by the fighting and cruel war which has divided Korea have died down, the parties will be able to meet again and renew discussions together," but the "time" so far elapsed has not been productive of any such action. It would appear that solutions can be accomplished only through a global showdown, a catastrophe no one wants to contemplate, or—more hopefully—through the long and painstaking negotiations of a greatly strengthened United Nations.

American Interests

The United States continues to carry its responsibilities in Korea, sometimes grudgingly and often without adequate understanding of Korean viewpoints. The Republic of Korea is not exactly a showplace of democracy nor of a free and expanding economy. American taxpayers grow weary of the large expenditure of funds to bolster the economy and to support the military forces necessary to defend the Republic of Korea from the continuous threat of Communist aggression.

The United States has had an active concern for the Republic of Korea only since 1945. Actually American entrance upon the Korean scene was not part of any grand design. At the Portsmouth (New Hampshire) Conference in 1905 the United States helped negotiate the ending of the Russo-Japanese War but did not actively seek to preserve Korea's independence. In subsequent years, the U. S. maintained a Consulate-General in Seoul, expressing little official concern over Japan's control of Korea. During World War II the United States participated with Great Britain and China in the Cairo Declaration (to which Russia later affirmed), which stated that "in due course" Korea would become independent. However, this declaration was aimed more at stripping Japan of her overseas empire than developing a strengthened Korea.

199

There was little political concern for Korea and scant study or training for an American military occupation there. Only one part of a civil affairs handbook (on agriculture) was prepared; language training was mainly for interrogators of prisoners-of-war. The State Department had virtually only one person, the author's brother, George M. McCune, working full time on Korean policies. Ill health made it necessary for him to resign during the summer of 1945 before the end of the war. The reasoning seemed to be that the Soviet Union, which had promised to enter the war against Japan, would likely be fighting on the mainland and that American troops would not be fighting in Korea. After the United States dropped atomic bombs on Japan precipitating a surrender, many decisions had to be made hastily. These included the imposing of the 38th parallel as a dividing line and the sending of American forces into Korea. Not all of Korea was allowed to fall to the Communist world by default, but the United States was not well prepared for its sudden responsibilities there.

Now, two decades later, and with the experience of the Korean War with its great American sacrifices behind us, American policy in Korea remains somewhat static. The keystone of that policy is to support the development of "a free, democratic and united Korea." But it is obvious that this will not be achieved quickly or with ease. With this long-range goal in mind, American policy is devoted to the preservation of the Republic of Korea built on a broad-based, growing economy and having, hopefully, a democratic outlook. America stands firmly against Communist aggression by remaining militarily vigilant and by furnishing military assistance to the ROK but at the same time insists that the South Korean government refrain from aggression against North Korea. The United States seeks to have the ROK work with the Japanese for peaceful solutions to their mutual problems. America's Korean policy is, thus, somewhat of a "holding operation." In spite of some Americans who call for a much more aggressive program even at the risk of a renewed war, the American position is to work toward solutions of the basic problems of Korea through the United Nations.

In contrast with the pre-World War II years when only a handful of Americans—businessmen, miners or missionaries— knew Korea first-hand, it is estimated that since 1945 over a million Americans have been stationed there for varying lengths of time. Almost all, however, were on military service and many found it less than enjoyable. As a consequence, few of these Americans have developed any great empathy for Korea or the Koreans (to state the case mildly!). The United States government, however, has granted more than $3,000,000,000 in aid to the ROK during the years. These grants have been a major bulwark to the Korean economy. Recently American private investment in Korea has increased but it is still small.

Some Americans, particularly those in military, diplomatic, and economic aid service, have developed a real understanding and appreciation of Korea. For instance, soldiers who have devoted long hours to rehabilitation projects in villages and towns have learned much in exchange. Some American scholars have worked in Korean universities and on research projects, often stimulating or helping Korean scholars to undertake basic research on Korea. Korean students have come to the United States to study, to remain in academic or scientific positions. Thousands of Korean girls who married American soldiers are now living in the United States, and many Korean orphans, including those of mixed blood, have been adopted into American homes. The small group of Koreans in Hawaii and California whose parents migrated sixty and seventy years ago strive to keep up interest in Korean culture. Missionaries returned to Korea to work with Korean Christian leaders, and missionaries of many faiths and backgrounds have joined them. The American-Korean Foundation, the Asia Foundation, and other foundations and societies, such as the Asia Society, have supported work in cultural, social science and scientific fields.

Still the average American on the street would rather forget about Korea. He thinks of it as a place of inconclusive warfare; he does not recognize the threat of the temporary Truce Line. To him Korea is a strange, faraway place of quaint and obstinate people, a land of rugged terrain where his cousin or uncle fought and, perhaps, died. This attitude toward Korea is hard to overcome. Yet it is damaging to the sound development of an American policy which will accomplish more than very limited objectives.

Soviet Russian Interests

This American attitude of remoteness from Korea and its problems is matched by a similar attitude on the part of the Russian people. Some Koreans had migrated to the Vladivostok area and then during World War II were moved en masse into central Asia. But they are not a significant element. Numerous Koreans attended Russian universities or underwent on-the-job training in Russian factories and farms, but most of them returned to North Korea. A small number of Russian and Korean scholars have been studying Korea and publishing books and articles on Korean subjects.

The Russians expected that their puppet Kim Ilsung and his followers would maintain close ties with the Soviet Union running the country as a Communist satellite. After an initial period of plunder, the economic policy was reversed and materials and funds flowed into Korea. The overall Russian policy was also for a united and "democratic" Korea. Seeing little progress being made towards unification and being

202

aware that some high American officials had proclaimed that Korea lay outside the periphery of American interests, the Russians urged and equipped the North Korean regime to launch its aggression to force unification in 1950.

As the Korean War turned against the aggressors, the Soviet Union did not pour in troops and equipment to reverse the trend, though they did urge the Chinese Communists to do so. When it looked as if the United States might be mounting a renewed offensive they took initiative to arrange for a truce. One can speculate that perhaps the Soviet Union has lived to regret the obvious consequences of Chinese Communist intervention in the Korean War for it resulted in the Soviet Union's influence in Korea being eclipsed by that of Communist China.

The Russian long-term aims continue to be a unified and subservient Korea, but they have had to be satisfied with much less—a divided Korea which they hope will continue to be an irritant to peace in the Far East, a drain on American resources. The Soviet Union continues to have cultural and limited economic ties with North Korea but they do not enjoy the political control they once exercised.

Communist China's Interest

For many centuries Imperial China's relation to Korea was that of an "elder brother," but eventually its power and influence dwindled and Japan took the ascendancy. The Chinese Nationalists gave some support to the "Provisional Government of Korea" in the 1920's and 30's and during the Japanese War, but this group which returned to Korea from Chungking had little real influence in post-World War II Korea. (Kim Ku, one-time President of the Provisional Government, was assassinated in Seoul in the summer of 1949.) A number of Koreans associated themselves with the Chinese

Communists in Yenan. When they returned to North Korea they were not a strong force and were eventually purged.

Communist Chinese interest in Korea is to be expected, for as a large nation it desires control over its small neighbor. However, it was not until the second phase of the Korean War that it had the power to exert real influence. When its economic and military interests were threatened by the approach of ROK and UN forces to the Yalu River, the Chinese Communists acted. Once firmly established in Korea they did not relinquish their control. Kim Ilsung quickly changed masters; particularly after the Soviet Union-Communist China ideological split, he cast his lot with the Chinese.

The Communist Chinese goals in Korea are simple and the same that China had had for centuries—to have a weak "younger brother" willing to take orders from and to make obeisance to the "older brother." They would like a unified Korea but are seemingly not willing to pay a large price for this. They dislike American "imperialists" in South Korea, but do not appear to fear aggression from them and constantly use the American presence as a propaganda theme to other Asian people. The Chinese Communists too, have their definition of a "democratic" nation, which is a totalitarian "strong-man" state. Though they have withdrawn the bulk of their troops, their forces are stationed close by in Manchuria. They are forging economic ties which will bind Korea even closer to China and which may make it eventually an economic province of China.

Japan's Interests

Japan is the only country of the world with a sizable Korean minority. The large numbers of Koreans who were formerly in China and Manchuria have gone back to Korea or been absorbed into Chinese society. A voluntary program of repatriation, organized through the Japanese Red Cross, moved some 170,000 Koreans from Japan to North Korea. But though hundreds of thousands of Koreans in Japan in 1945 were repatriated, there still remain a significant number, perhaps a half million, of Korean ancestry. The Korean minority in Japan is a very interesting group. Many of these Koreans are leftist or under leftist control. Many have been living in slum-like areas of Japanese cities and have been engaged in black market and similar activities. They have aroused considerable antagonism among the Japanese, creating as they do severe problems for the Japanese authorities. Though it may seem illogical, the Koreans have claimed both immunities as foreigners and special privileges because of the Japanese oppression of Korea. The handling of the Korean minority is a major source of friction between Japan and the ROK.

Japan, as a close neighbor and as the former colonial ruler, has no clear-cut policy in regard to Korea. Taking into account American political pressure and Japanese economic desires, Japan has sought to stabilize its relationships with the Republic of Korea. It would like to see a unified Korea but is realistically not expecting this to occur in the immediate future. There is a large and vocal leftist group of Japanese which presses for relationships with North Korea equivalent to those with the ROK. The present government does not respond to this pressure. In the treaty initiated in the spring of 1965 with the ROK, the Japanese recognized it as "the only government" in Korea, following the UN precedent.

The Japanese resented the intransigence of the ROK under Syngman Rhee. They sometimes openly assumed a superior attitude and this in turn was deeply resented by the Koreans. Many Japanese had been in Korea before World War II, but as colonial masters. They have had difficulty changing their personal attitudes toward Koreans, whom they considered (and treated) as second class persons. More recently, the Japanese

205

have become more conciliatory to match a softening Korean attitude, for they are anxious to obtain access to the fishing grounds beyond the Rhee Line as well as opportunities for investment in Korea. They would like to see a democratic and stable government in Korea with which they could carry on mutually profitable trade.

Many capable Japanese scholars are engaged in Korean studies. The *Chosen Gakuho* (Korean Studies), a journal published by the *Chosen Gakkai* (The Association of Koreanology in Japan), has an excellent collection of learned articles and keeps clear of political affairs. A new generation of Japanese scholars exists which views Korea with objectivity and some appreciation of its cultural heritage, which was a source of enrichment to Japanese culture in past centuries.

ROK-DPRK Relations

The governments of North and South Korea are bitterly opposed to each other. They have developed under different auspices and in different political frameworks. They have met on fields of battle that ranged widely up and down the peninsula. Now each has poised on its side of the Truce Line military forces of roughly a half million men. It is obvious that peace and unification of Korea will only come with the defeat of or a drastic change in the character of one or the other. Both governments maintain as a basic policy the re-unification of their land. Both carry on programs to preserve the Korean identity. Both seek to improve the economic conditions of their people. However, they differ decidedly in the manner in which these aims should be accomplished.

The Korean War is a bitter memory to the Korean people on both sides of the Truce Line. They fear a renewal of the war and the resultant devastation. The sixteen nations which came to the aid of the ROK in 1950 have clearly stated that in the event of a resumption of the war it would not be confined to the Korean peninsula and, by inference, to conventional weapons. Thus it is not likely that the Chinese Communists and the Soviet Union will urge (as they did in 1950) the DPRK to engage in an offensive across the Truce Line. Both governments are vigilant in their defense, and both engage in unceasing propaganda and psychological warfare.

In the Republic of Korea there is an important group of people, the refugees from North Korea, who are anxious to return to their own part of Korea. They have not been totally assimilated into the ROK and are apt to congregate in certain sectors of Seoul and other cities. They have some of their own institutions, for example, Christian churches. They are an extremely important force in keeping active the pressure for unification. During the freer atmosphere of the Chang regime some public expression of a desire for reconciliation and peaceful negotiation was heard.

In North Korea, one hears constant appeals for the withdrawal of "American imperialists" from South Korea. Constituting less than a third of the total Korean population, the DPRK would obviously be the loser in any free elections. Outsiders have advocated some form of federation, but this is scarcely feasible between two governments, one of which is a totalitarian Communist state and the other a free nation groping toward a representative form of government.

The United Nations and Korea

When in 1947 the United States found itself at an impasse with the Soviet Union it presented the Korean problem to the United Nations. Since then numerous UN commissions, committees, and agencies have been involved in Korean affairs. Their voluminous reports make interesting reading despite their dull format. The UN has taken its responsibilities seriously. In 1948 a temporary UN Commission reported on the formation of a constitution and the holding of elections in South Korea. The UN General Assembly then named the ROK as a lawful government and the only such government in Korea. The UN Security Council labeled the North Koreans as aggressors in 1950. (The Soviet Union was staging one of its walkouts at the time.) This action and the subsequent UN appeal for military forces was a major turning point for the United Nations. It showed itself as more than just a debating society; now it was acting and willing to use military force to deter aggression. In December, 1950, the UN set up a Korean Reconstruction Agency to carry out an aid program in Korea. From then until 1959 when it ceased operations, UNKRA expended $150,000,000 on projects in Korea. In addition the specialized agencies of the UN, such as UNESCO, FAO, WHO, and UNICEF, have been carrying on programs in education, agriculture, health, and child welfare in Korea.

In recent years the UN General Assembly and its committees have often placed the Korean problem on their agenda. The basic aim of the UN is for a unified, independent, and democratic Korea under a representative form of government. However, in view of the inability of the UN Commissions to enter North Korea and with both Communist China and North Korea officially called aggressors by the UN, the chances for this aim to be achieved are dim.

The United States and other free nations have supported UN activities in Korea, while the Soviet Union and members of its bloc have consistently opposed them. A United Nations increased in strength so that it can effectively exercise power is the major hope for a peaceful resolution of the Korean problem. Unfortunately the prerequisite strengthening of the United Nations is a long and slow process. In the meantime, the increasingly rigid division of Korea by the Truce Line and the increasingly divergent developments of governments in North and South Korea do not warrant any optimism for the early realization of a free, democratic, unified Korea.

Friends of Korea and the Koreans must take solace in the abiding nature of this land of high mountains and sparkling streams, in the enduring qualities of mind and spirit possessed by the Korean people, and in the hope that some peaceful morning the calm, now broken, will be restored.

Further Reading on Korea

Below are listed some books and journals in English that may be of interest for further reading on Korea. Some of these have bibliographical references. A most useful current bibliography is the section on Korea in the annual "Bibliography of Asian Studies" in the *Journal of Asian Studies* published by the Association for Asian Studies.

CHUNG, KYUNG-CHO. *New Korea: New Land of the Morning Calm.* New York: The Macmillan Co., 1962.

Documents of the Fourth Congress of the Workers' Party of Korea. Pyongyang: Foreign Language Publishing House, 1961.

Education in Korea. Seoul: Ministry of Education and National Commission for UNESCO, 1962.

FEHRENBACH, T. R. *This Kind of War.* New York: The Macmillan Co., 1963.

GOODRICH, LELAND M. *Korea—A Study of U. S. Policy in the United Nations.* New York: Council on Foreign Relations, 1956.

HAZARD, B. H., JR., JAMES HOYT, H. T. KIM and W. W. SMITH, JR. *Korean Studies Guide.* Berkeley: University of California Press, 1954.

Journal of Social Sciences and Humanities. Seoul: Bulletin of The Korean Research Center, since 1955.

KANG, YOUNGHILL. *The Grass Roof.* New York: Charles Scribner's Sons, 1931.

KEITH, ELIZABETH and E. K. ROBERTSON SCOTT. *Old Korea: The Land of Morning Calm.* London: Hutchinson & Co., Ltd., 1946.

Korea: Its Land, People and Culture of All Ages. Seoul: Hakwon-sa, 1960.

Korean Affairs. Seoul: The Council on Korean Affairs, quarterly since 1962.

Koreana Quarterly. Seoul: The International Research Centre, quarterly since 1959.

LEE, CHONG-SIK. *The Politics of Korean Nationalism.* Berkeley: University of California Press, 1963.

LEE, PETER H. *Anthology of Korean Poetry from the Earliest Era to the Present.* New York: The John Day Co., 1964.

———. *Korean Literature: Topics and Themes.* Tucson: University of Arizona Press for the Association for Asian Studies, 1965.

MARSHALL, S. L. A. *The River and the Gauntlet.* New York: William Morrow & Co., 1953.

McCUNE, EVELYN. *The Arts of Korea, An Illustrated History.* Rutland, Vermont: Charles E. Tuttle Co., 1962.

McCUNE, GEORGE M., with the collaboration of ARTHUR L. GREY, JR. *Korea Today.* Cambridge: Harvard University Press, 1950.

McCUNE, SHANNON. *Korea's Heritage, A Regional and Social Geography.* Rutland, Vermont: Charles E. Tuttle Co., 1956.

NELSON, M. FREDERICK. *Korea and the Old Orders in Eastern Asia.* Baton Rouge: Louisiana State University Press, 1946.

OSGOOD, CORNELIUS. *The Koreans and Their Culture.* New York: The Ronald Press, 1951.

REEVE, W. D. *The Republic of Korea, A Political and Economic Study.* London: Oxford University Press, 1963.

Rehabilitation and Development of Agriculture, Forestry, and Fisheries in South Korea. New York: Columbia University Press,. 1954.

RUTT, RICHARD. *Korean Works and Days.* Rutland, Vermont: Charles E. Tuttle Co., 1964.

SCALAPINO, ROBERT A., ed. *North Korea Today.* New York: Frederick A. Praeger, 1963.

The Korean Studies Series. Seoul: The Korean Research Center, since 1955.

UNESCO Korean Survey. Compiled by The Korean National Commission for UNESCO. Seoul: Dong-a Publishing Co., 1960.

ZONG, IN-SOB. *Folk Tales from Korea.* London: Routledge & Kegan Paul Ltd., 1952.

211

Index

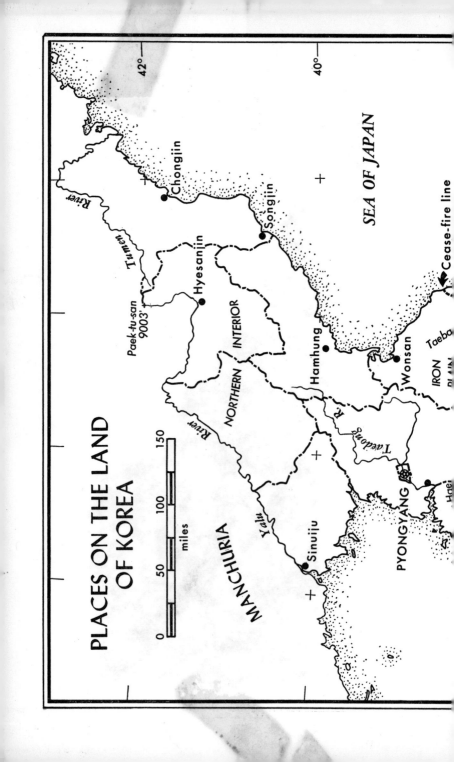

PLACES ON THE LAND OF KOREA

MANCHURIA

Tumen River

Paek-tu-san 9003'

Chongjin

Songjin

Hyesanjin

NORTHERN INTERIOR

Hamhung

Yalu River

Sinuiju

SEA OF JAPAN

Cease-fire line

Wonsan

Taeba

IRON

Taedong R.

PYONGYANG

Hae

42°

40°

miles

0   50   100   150